The publishers would like to thank the following companies for their

support in the production of this book

Main Sponsor

Warburtons

WM Allen

Anthony Axford Limited

S C Chadwick

CMP Batteries Limited

George Cox & Sons

Engineering Service Co

Walter Forshaw

Gregory & Porritts

H J Grundy

Harker & Howarth Music Limited

Kemax Tools Limited

Manfredi (Bolton) Limited

Market Hall

Bernard Stott Decorators

Richard Threlfall

Whittakers Shoemakers

First published in Great Britain by True North Books Limited
England HX5 9AE
01422 377977

ISBN 1 903204 37 2

Text, design and origination by True North Books Limited
Printed and bound by The Amadeus Press Limited

Bolton Memories

Contents

Introduction

elcome to 'Bolton Memories'. This book is the latest in a series that revisits the town that our parents and grandparents knew so well. Older readers will recall many of the forgotten scenes for themselves. Younger ones will be able to put in place the sights and sounds of 20th century Bolton that they were told about with such affection. This new collection of delightful photographs brings back to life a time when the pace of life was so different. There really was an age when mobile phones did not disturb the peace of the lounge bar in the pub. Once upon a time we had individual and speciality shops; we can see some of them again inside this book. Supermarkets and shopping malls, ugly concrete office blocks and super fast highways were still to come when many of these images were captured. Each one is accompanied by thoughtful captions which contain a mixture of fact and reminiscence. All of them are presented with one aim in mind, that of creating a mood of nostalgia for those days that are far behind us. The book makes no apology for indulging in that warm glow of reflecting on the past, times have changed, not always for the better. However, not everything new is to be dismissed as a lowering of standards, 'Bolton Memories' will also remind the reader of wartime days, when we feared the worst as bombers flew overhead on missions to Manchester, Salford and Liverpool. Those were the times when food, fuel and clothing were rationed, when thousands went off to fight the enemy and many did not return. There was the depression of the early 1930s and the austere times of postwar Britain. We had few electrical aids in our kitchens and housework was drudgery. We have left those days behind, but they are not forgotten, they have to be recalled to gain a balance when we celebrate the happier times. 'Bolton Memories' will help bring to life those merrier occasions, made all the more poignant by recalling that it was not all sweetness and light. However, we can be forgiven for concentrating on the events, activities and sheer joie de vivre that has made Bolton such a special place.

The Women's Junior Air Corps on parade in August 1944.

Continued from previous page: This famous old Lancashire town became part of the new Greater Manchester County in 1974, following local government reorganisation. When the county council was done away with in 1986 the borough gained a greater control of its own life and destiny. Nowadays it includes a number of outlying towns and villages within its 54 square miles and boasts a population of around 270,000. This book concentrates on drawing upon photographs of when Bolton was still as Lancashire as pigs' trotters, tripe and flat caps. It looks at street scenes when Japanese, Korean, French and German cars were a rarity, look carefully and you might be able to spot a Morris Cowley or Hillman Imp making its way along Bradshawgate.

But Bolton has had more to offer down the centuries than just being another northern town. It has more importance in the history of Britain than the development of the black pudding. As with most settlements, the first roots of the modern town grew in a valley, close to a ready water supply. Known as Bolton-le-Moors because of the West Pennine moorland close by, the early settlement took shape on the banks of the River Croal. There is evidence of Bronze Age development in the area, but the existence of Bolton Manor was first recorded in 1212. By then, Bolton was well known for its local textiles. Long before cotton was king, the sheep grazing on the windswept moors provided fleeces that helped build a flourishing cottage industry, producing woollen goods. About 1100, Richard the Lionheart had heard enough about the skills of local craftsmen to send royal officials north to check the quality of the cloth. Cotton was introduced in the 17th century, but the textile industry still developed slowly. It was not until the following century, when mechanisation was introduced, that the boom years began; by then cotton had replaced wool as the main raw material. In 1779, a native of Bolton, Samuel Crompton, invented the spinning mule, it revolutionised the industry and Bolton's first spinning mill was opened in 1780. By the mid-19th century the town had grown to become an important centre, not just for textiles, but coal mining, papermaking, bleaching, engineering and a range of other industries. Although the cotton industry contracted in the last century, there were still nearly 250 cotton mills in operation in 1929. It is from around that time that 'Bolton Memories' takes its first steps along memory lane. As the reader starts to leaf

A busy scene in Newport Street on a cold and wet December day, 1955.

through the opening pages entrance is made to a world where bullseyes were sweets and not a direct hit from a vandal's brick. Britain was a land where paperboys whistled the pop songs of the day, 'rap' was a knock on the door, not some tuneless mumbling of a performer who cannot sing a note. Schoolchildren sat in rows at their desks and gave up their seats on buses to adults, shop assistants saw it their duty to serve with a smile and knew the words 'please' and 'thank you'. AA motorcyclists saluted their members as they drove past. Cinemas showed two films for the price of one and there were no fast food cartons littering the streets. Bobbies on the beat, Dan Dare on the wireless and tortoiseshell plastic hair slides for the twin with the Toni perm. These are the sort of memories that will come flooding back as you wade through page after page of sheer nostalgia. We had the Lion of Vienna, Nat Lofthouse, frightening the life out of the opposition up and down the country. Remember when Burnden Park saw centre forwards not strikers and stoppers were what you put in the neck of your bottle of Tizer?

Perhaps the best way to read 'Bolton Memories' is to get into true nostalgic mood. Go to the wardrobe and select an A-line skirt or pair of drainpipe trousers. Put in a set of curlers or slick back your hair with a dab of Brylcreem. Tell the children to close their copies of 'School Friend' and 'Film Fun' and tidy away the Biggles and Famous Five books. Wind up the gramophone and put on an old 78. Anne Shelton can sing 'Arrivederci Darling' or Johnny Ray belt out 'Such a Night'. Fill the pot with some Horniman's tea and pop it under the little cosy that grandma knitted. Reach for a plateful of sugar butties and you are ready for the off. It is now the moment to return to the Lido Cinema or the Imperial Playhouse for your Saturday night out. Come with us again to the Brown Cow and Commercial Hotel, hop on a chara during the June holiday week and take that short journey to the Golden Mile at Blackpool once more. Drive a Ford Prefect through Victoria Square and recall shopping at Salisbury's, Price's and the Corset Shop on Newport Street. All this and more await you as you turn the first page. As they say in modern restaurants, 'Enjoy'.

Street scenes

Bradshawgate was no place for the faint hearted in early 1940. The fierce snows of that winter had come with a vengeance. In these days of global warming we have forgotten how severe our climate could be. Deep snowdrifts and biting winds made it uncomfortable and difficult to get around. Men wielding shovels cleared a pathway for the few cars venturing onto the streets. We helped ourselves in those days, rather than wait for the council to provide snowploughs. The couple making its way past the bank looks frozen stiff. They would have come from houses that did not have the benefit of central heating at the flick of a switch. On such chilly days families got dressed in front of the embers of the living room fire, still warm from the night before. If they used cars or buses to travel into work or off to school, there was little chance of heaters blowing hot air across their icy feet. Yorkshire Penny Bank, on the left, was established in 1859, though it did not appear on Bradshawgate until 70 years later. The building had been home to Fletcher's, a hatter in business there since the middle of the 19th century. The bank was rebuilt in 1933, on this corner of Wood Street. It dropped the 'Penny' in its title in the 1950s.

In 1934 Bolton town centre still showed evidence that the roots of its prosperity were fixed in the industrial revolution. Warehouses and the chimneys of factories and mills can be seen close to the railway lines that brought in the raw materials and took away the finished goods. The photograph shows Trinity Street and Bradshawgate, with Bury Road running towards the top right corner. The railway line on the left sweeps away to the north. The importance of the railway to the cotton trade can be measured by the volume of cloth that was moved in the years either side of its coming. What had been less than 300 million yards being exported from Lancashire in the early 19th century had increased sevenfold by 1860. Bolton's first goods line opened two years earlier than that of the Manchester to Liverpool line. The Bolton to Leigh line opened in 1828. By 1840 the network system around Bolton was complete. This was well before the rest of the country and the town stole a march on others, enabling it to get off to a flying start ahead of its competitors. Trinity Street is now Bolton's main town centre railway station. In 1987 it moved to the other side of the street during its facelift. It is now combined with the Newport street bus-rail interchange.

Below: In the early 1930s people's eyes seemed to be permanently in shadow. The large peaks on flat hats and the brims on homburgs created the effect for men. Women pulled down the cloche hats on their heads with the same result. This set of locals stood in front of the statue of Samuel Crompton in Nelson Square. It was built by public subscription and unveiled by the mayor, JP Wolfenden, in 1862. It honours the Firwood inventor of a device that permitted large scale manufacture of high-quality thread and yarn. As it was a cross between the inventions of Richard Arkwright and James Hargreaves' spinning jenny, he called it a spinning mule.

Crompton's invention brought him fame but no wealth. He died a pauper in 1827 and is buried in St Peter's churchyard. A 1998 pub, to the left of the statue, is called the Spinning Mule in Crompton's memory. The war memorial, on the left, marks 'the glorious memory' of the Bolton Artillery. Behind it stood the old education offices, demolished in 1972, that had once been Bolton Infirmary, a small seven bed hospital. The Levers Arms, also called the Cock and Trumpet, was to the right of Crompton until it closed in 1949. Three years later the Pack Horse Hotel, next door, was extended over this site and further developed in 1962.

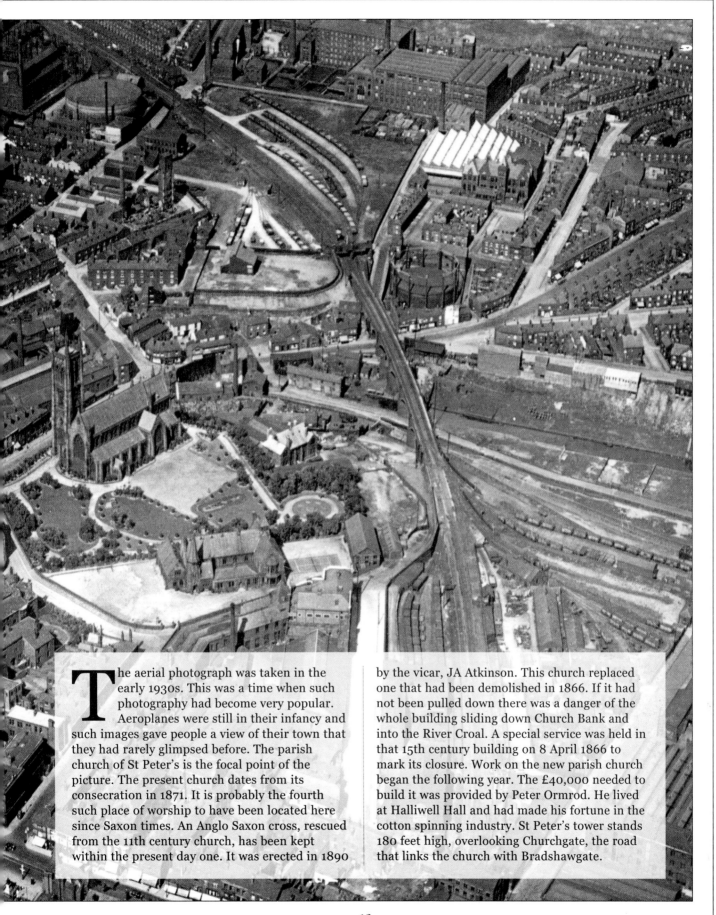

The aerial photograph was taken in the early 1930s. This was a time when such photography had become very popular. Aeroplanes were still in their infancy and such images gave people a view of their town that they had rarely glimpsed before. The parish church of St Peter's is the focal point of the picture. The present church dates from its consecration in 1871. It is probably the fourth such place of worship to have been located here since Saxon times. An Anglo Saxon cross, rescued from the 11th century church, has been kept within the present day one. It was erected in 1890 by the vicar, JA Atkinson. This church replaced one that had been demolished in 1866. If it had not been pulled down there was a danger of the whole building sliding down Church Bank and into the River Croal. A special service was held in that 15th century building on 8 April 1866 to mark its closure. Work on the new parish church began the following year. The £40,000 needed to build it was provided by Peter Ormrod. He lived at Halliwell Hall and had made his fortune in the cotton spinning industry. St Peter's tower stands 180 feet high, overlooking Churchgate, the road that links the church with Bradshawgate.

Below: The Queen's was one of the three cinemas to have been established on Bradshawgate, over the years. This view of it is from the junction with Trinity Street. The cinema, once known as the Queen's Picture Hall, was built on part of Clarence Yard. When it opened on 2 December 1912 silent movies were often accompanied by music played by a pianist, seated in a pit below the screen. The ivories were tinkled to help set the mood for the film. Stirring chords were played to accompany stirring deeds and moments of high drama. Delicate, smooth touches were brought to bear at more romantic moments, as when the screen vamp Theda Bara lured men to their destruction. Audiences flocked to see her in 'Camille' and 'Cleopatra' in those early days. The Queen's opened with a greater flourish than just providing a pianist. A full orchestra accompanied the film. Now, that was real class. The admission charges reflected it. They were pricey for pre first world war times. The cheapest seats were 3d and it cost a shilling for the best ones. This compared with just a tanner (6d) in other picture houses. In January 1953 Theda Bara's star had long waned. Elizabeth Taylor was now one of the hottest names around. She was one of the few to make the transition from child star to top billing as an adult. Now nearly 21, she was appearing alongside Joan Fontaine and opposite Robert Taylor in the screen version of Sir Walter Scott's epic 'Ivanhoe'. The Queen's closed in July 1966. It became a bingo hall in 1969 and began showing Asian films in the 1970s. It has since been demolished and the site used as a car showroom.

Right: Water Street is one of the little back streets now marooned in a triangle created by Churchgate, Folds Road and St Peter's Way. Today, it backs on to a piece of waste land used as a car park. In 1955 it was home to two little girls who had been born into an austere lifestyle as Britain tried to recover from the second world war. In their toddler years their mums still had to use ration books to buy their food and clothing allowance.

Botttom: This section of Newport Street runs from Trinity Street to Great Moor Street. The post office is on the corner with Back Newport Street. By 1957 the country had started to leave behind the grim days that followed the war. Bomb damaged areas had been cleared and new enterprises begun. In our homes we were experiencing an electrical revolution; fridges, washing machines, vacuum cleaners and televisions were becoming much more commonplace.

Rationing was not completely lifted until 1954. The children had often heard their dads mutter about who really won this war. Such talk was beyond their understanding. They were wrapped up in a world of hopscotch and spinning tops. The girls knocked over sticks and ran and hid in a game of rally-o. Later they played two ball against the wall, chanting 'Matthew, Mark, Luke and John; Acts and Romans, follow on'. At the top of the hill members of the Conservative Club knew the highs and lows of political life. At the end of the war the public dumped Churchill in favour of Clement Attlee's Labour government. In 1951 they raised their glasses to good old Winnie as the country returned him to power. His era in politics came to an end in the year this photograph was taken. In 1955 Conservatives welcomed their new leader, Anthony Eden. The girls went to look for their skipping ropes.

Monday washday and house cleaning was easier for the housewife. Family entertainment centred upon that little picture box in the corner of the living room. We had two TV channels to choose from. BBC newsreaders still dressed formally and that channel provided a lot of serious programmes and drama. The brash mix of game shows and light entertainment offered by ITV challenged it. Rationing was behind us. It had ended three years ago. We had a brighter future ahead. Our sportsmen were stars. Derek Ibbotson broke the world record for running the mile. Mike Hawthorn and Stirling Moss led the way in motor racing. We had fast bowlers in Freddie Trueman and Brian Statham who could skittle out batsmen and Chelsea gave a debut to a 17 year old soccer player called Jimmy Greaves. Prime Minister Macmillan told us that we had never had it so good in a famous speech in July. How right he was.

Above: Alec Issigonis designed the Morris Minor in 1948. In 1959 he followed up this success with the Mini, the fuel efficient answer to the VW Beetle. British cars dominated our streets. The invasion by Nissan, Toyota, Honda and other Far East manufacturers had still to come. Examples of Issigonis' designs can be seen dotted around this 1965 view of Victoria Square. So famous did his Minis become that the cars became the best remembered part of the 1969 movie, 'The Italian Job'. The 1960s was a decade of great change in our society. The austere postwar years were well behind us. Unemployment was low and we had money burning a hole in our pockets. Car ownership became commonplace. Our petrol prices were amongst the lowest in Europe. How that has changed! The voice of young people was heard more loudly. The teenager became a valued consumer. He demanded his own fashions, both in clothing and in lifestyle. All this under the watchful eye of the sculpture on the left. The lion is one of the magnificent pair that guards the town hall steps. Leo seems to be gazing at the Commercial Hotel that stood there from Georgian times. Perhaps he fancied a pint of Magee's. The Commercial closed in April 1972 and was demolished later that year. Mothercare took over the site in August 1974.

In June 1958 reconstruction work was well under way on the buildings of the Co-operative Society and the extension to Woolworth's. The Co-op had been here since the mid 19th century. It had been a series of small, separate shops, before being turned into a single, larger establishment. It was reconstructed into a supermarket. By the 1990s this area of Bridge Street was remodelled once more. A fish market stood on this street until it was knocked down in 1933. In the early days of the Co-op, the Woolworth building was used by a funeral director, Constantine Brothers. Woolworth's took over the site in 1926. It opened its doors to customers on 27 November, just in time for the run up to Christmas. The premises were once known as Britannia House, because of the statue that was on top, but that was removed in 1942. The scaffolding seen here stayed until the building work was completed in 1959. Bridge Street was built to cross the River Croal. In Georgian times the river acted as the boundary between Little Bolton and Great Bolton. That changed in January 1838 when the two councils got together. They drew up a charter of incorporation. Queen Victoria granted the newly combined Bolton chartered borough status on 11 October 1838. James Darbishire was elected as Bolton's first mayor a month later.

As you drive along Great Moor Street today, close to Soho Street, it is likely that you will crawl your way through the sets of traffic lights. It is a busy spot. In 1962 movement was much easier. The days of heavy congestion were still to come. The motor scooter was one of the symbols of that time, now 40 years ago. Lambretta and Vespa were popular models that became a statement of culture as well as a means of transport. By the middle of the swinging 60s there were rival camps of two wheel society. Young people divided into groups known as Mods and Rockers. The latter clung to the music and hairstyles of the 1950s. They went for burn ups on their high powered motorbikes, often 'doing a ton' as

they topped 100 mph. They dressed in black leather and collected Gene Vincent and Eddie Cochran records. The duffel coated Mods, with their long, clean hair, were the sworn enemy. Their music was all Marmalade and Small Faces. No Bank Holiday was complete without a seaside clash between the two factions. They could have prepared for the fray with a few pints of Watney's Red Barrel at the Flag Hotel right through the decade. However, that opportunity would disappear in 1970 when the pub closed. The site is now used as a car park. It seems odd today that those Mods and Rockers are looking forward to when they qualify for a bus pass, rather than planning the next punch up on the sands.

Above: This part of Newport Street and Victoria Square were photographed before the area was pedestrianised. Then, Ford Anglias and buses motored freely along the road, not realising that the days of open access to this part of Bolton were soon to disappear. Shopping became a much more pleasant experience in this part of town. It had been an exercise in dodging between lines of traffic when trying to cross the road. The smell and smoke from car exhausts made it an unhealthy experience as well. Traffic ground to a halt and frustrated drivers tooted one another in the idiotic belief that the noise would clear the jam. Now, strolling along Newport Street and into the Square, is a much more relaxed and pleasant way to do your shopping. Some of us even just go for a walk along there or to window shop, without the worry of the problems created by the internal combustion engine. We can even take a look at the various elephants, quaintly dotted around here and in other parts of the town. There is a pair of magnificent cast iron beasts on the canopy in Victoria Square that once adorned the gates of the old Bolton Bleachworks. The elephant was incorporated into the Coat of Arms in 1890. Images of 'Jumbo' appear on banks, bins, bollards and bridges.

Below: The roundabout is at the junction of Moss Bank Way and Chorley Old Road, the B6226 that leads away past Delph Hill Mill. Bolton had once been covered with mills, weaving sheds and bleaching works. Cheap imports from the Far East in the 1950s and the introduction of artificial fibres sounded the death knell for the textile industry. By the time of the swinging 60s, when these boys waited for their school bus, future employment for them in cotton was most unlikely. By the time they left school or university it would be local authorities and service industries that provided the greatest job opportunities. These youngsters were growing up in a decade of changing attitudes as well. Their big sisters burned their bras and joined older brothers on peace marches in an effort to ban the bomb. They rejected much of the old order, refusing to follow blindly the orders of the establishment. Soon, these schoolboys would follow that example. They would discard their silly school caps. They laughed about the days when the prefects met them off the bus and fined them sixpence for not wearing them. Those caps and short trousers were seen as a symbol of conforming. Individuality became their ethic. They threw their short trousers onto the same fire their big sisters had used.

The market in Ashburner Street was very busy in 1972. But that was nothing new. It had been so for 40 years, since it opened in 1932. Many stallholders took advantage of the new building, moving from the old Market Hall that had been in place since 1855. Both markets continue to flourish today. This one, close to Moor Lane bus station, is well known for the quality of its fruit and vegetables and boasts a well renowned fish market. The old Market Hall in Knowsley Street, modernised in 1938, has a number of specialist shops in addition to its market stalls. Bolton received its first charter to hold a market in Churchgate from King Henry III in 1251 when bartering would have been used as much as the groat. When this scene was captured the great British public was still trying to come to terms with what it called 'new money'. Tanners, shillings, florins and half crowns were no more. They became 2.5p, 5p, 10p and 12.5p. On 15 February 1971 Britain had its peacetime D-Day. Decimal coinage was introduced. For a while the old coinage existed alongside the new. Many older people were confused and could not take to the change. Gradually we got used to it, but old habits die hard. Some stallholders insisted on keeping the terms they had always used and sold goods for 30 bob rather than £1.50.

At leisure

Moss Bank Park is a lovely place to relax away from the hustle and bustle of everyday life. These days it hosts Animal World and Butterfly House. There is a miniature railway, old English garden, kiddies' play area and the rock garden. Soccer, cricket and tennis are regularly played there. The putting and bowling greens are still used, just as they were in 1934 when these two young lovelies demonstrated their golfing prowess while the menfolk got on with their game of 'old man's marbles'. The winsome lass on the left was making sure that her hair was just so as she posed for the photographer. She need not have worried. She was as pretty as a picture. Her blonde friend was no less appealing. They must have turned a few heads in their time. They belonged to a period of our history when women were coming out from behind the kitchen sink to play a more equal role with men. In 1928 they had, at last, been given full voting rights. Women started to play a more active role in the workplace. In sport they were no longer kept in the background. Gone were the days when they were expected to giggle and tap a ball gently with a racket or stick while men played the game properly. Women like Joyce Wethered and Dorothy Round led the way. Joyce was the Surrey golfer who toured America as a professional player. Dorothy was winning the Wimbledon tennis title for Britain at the very moment our pair of beauties was sinking its putts in Moss Bank Park.

The rock gardens in Moss Bank Park were just coming back to life on 22 March 1937. The early blooms had opened after the winter frosts to herald the coming of spring. Crocuses and snowdrops provided a beautiful backdrop for the tiny tots to enjoy the reflections cast in the rock pool. Their happy, if slightly chilled, faces were a joy to behold. It was a peaceful place to enjoy a family outing under the watery sun. It had officially become a park in 1922. The youngsters were having a whale of a time, feeling the grass under their feet and, later on, playing on the swings. Then it was off home for a warm drink and a game of Ludo or Snakes and Ladders. On the way there perhaps they stopped off at the sweetshop for a bag of sherbet or stick of licorice. Maybe they paid with the new coin introduced that year. A 12 sided threepenny bit made its entrance into our purses. It was minted to replace the old 'silver joey' that we used to put inside our Christmas puddings. How many of those ended up inside our tummies instead of on our pudding plates? Their demise gave us a taste of inflation. As the silver 3d piece was phased out we had to use 6d tanners in our puddings instead. The children did not complain. They gleefully put the coins they had not swallowed into their piggy banks.

Below: These are some of the children of the baby boomer years. Now summertime in 1954, they came into the world in those immediate postwar years when families were reunited. It was not a joyous time for everyone. The divorce rate went through the roof. Marriages had been put under immense pressure by the separations created by the war. Not everyone waited faithfully. But, for those who did, the reunions were all the more tender. When couples got back together a gal has to do what a gal has to do! The stork put in for overtime and Farley's sold out of rusks. This happy little band of nippers was enjoying its afternoon in Moss Bank Park. Perhaps they had a boat to sail or some ducks to feed. By now they will be thinking about early retirement, but what would they give to turn the clock back to those days in the park? Can they recall the simple joys of that era of their lives? The sun shone and they did not have a care in the world. Maybe they remember this day because of the little scamp behind them. What has he got in those jars? Is it some frogspawn or a few tiddlers he has fished out of the pond? Was this the occasion when he tiptoed forward and emptied the lot over the girls' heads? Oh yes, we remember it well.

Lancastrian Georgie Fame once sang 'Sitting in the park'. Over 20 years before he released that song Bolton folk showed that they could do more than just sit around. They danced in the park. In the summer of 1943, during Bolton holiday week, they strutted their wartime version of today's funky stuff on the grass of Moss Bank Park. And they did it in style. This was not boogying on down to the disco beat. This was proper dancing. The waltz, quickstep and foxtrot meant that you could glide across the turf with the same elegance used on the boards of the dance hall. This was the era of the big bands. American GIs helped popularise the music of Benny Goodman, Harry James, the Dorseys and Glenn Miller. We had Joe Loss, Ted Heath and the more refined Henry Hall. With the funfair and sideshows in the background, dancers displayed their talent for spin turns, chassis glides and lock steps. The more energetic threw themselves and their partners around in the jitterbug. Hit tunes sung by Patti, Laverne and Maxene, the Andrews Sisters, went down well. 'Boogie-woogie bugle boy' and 'Don't sit under the apple tree' got everyone on their feet, as did Glenn Miller's 'Little brown jug'. Sadly, many girls had to dance with their own sex. So many men were away at the front. But they could still enjoy the dance, even if it was not quite the same as having a boy in your arms.

Below: It was the September holiday week in 1947, at the end of one of the best summers on record. Factories and mills closed across the town as Bolton emptied. 'Charas' and trains were full with holidaymakers off to the seaside for seven days of fun. Saucy McGill postcards would be sent to relatives, telling tales of donkey rides on the sands. 'Wish you were here' was written on nearly every one, whether it was meant or not. Moor Lane bus station was crowded with people and their luggage. Blackpool, Rhyl and Prestatyn were popular destinations. The nights were taken up by visits to the summer shows where variety acts kept audiences hugely entertained. There was dancing at the Tower Ballroom and in the Winter Gardens. They stayed in guesthouses run by fierce landladies who served

breakfast at eight o'clock sharp. Heaven help the family that was late down. The wrath of the proprietor was awesome. Then, hail, rain or shine, guests were turfed out onto the streets and only let back in for the evening meal. To think we paid good money for the privilege! Posher folk went to Lytham St Annes or to take the waters at Harrogate. They usually stayed in hotels where the service was more geared to the customer. However, they did not come back with stories about fearsome dragons that the rest of us could tell.

Bottom: Nowadays it is all Majorca, Disneyland and the Greek islands. We make arrangements for the taxi to take us to Manchester Airport and then it is off on the jet for two weeks in the sun. This 1967 scene on platform two at Trinity Street station was before that type of holiday became commonplace. Foreign travel and package tours were with us, but for many a week or two at a British resort was still the norm for the annual holiday. We padded out our breaks with day trips by rail or charabanc. During Bolton holiday weeks the excursion specials to the Fylde coast and North Wales were kept very busy. Trinity Street station echoed with the noisy hubbub of voices chattering in eager anticipation of the journey ahead. It heralded a change from the daily grind of the workplace or the boredom of housework. In the 60s it became less fashionable for women to wear a hat. Once they would not have been seen dead without some form of headgear. Those who still raided their hatboxes made sure they picked a smart one to go with their holiday outfit. As demand for rail travel declined, the station was demolished. A smaller station on Newport Street replaced it, though the old clock tower was kept as a reminder of the days when thousands passed through Trinity Street on a daily basis.

Young mums, toddlers and old men were enjoying the sunshine in Bridgeman Park. The grassy slopes were good spots to indulge in a little sunbathing. In those days hemlines reflected the country's prosperity. During the war money and material were scarce, so skirts were shorter. By June 1958 we were in the Macmillan 'never had it so good' years. The economy was booming, unemployment was becoming a thing of the past and we had cash in our purses to spare. Hemlines dropped lower and lower. Girls wore them over petticoats that crackled as they walked. They made a pretty sight when twirling on the dance floor as they billowed out in the jive. It was not until the sexual revolution of the next decade that skirt lengths abandoned their links with wealth. Otherwise, Mary Quant's mini skirt would have meant the country was bankrupt! The lovely pram in the centre of the picture would have been that mum's pride and joy. She would have lavished as much attention on its appearance as any motorist would on his Morris Minor or Ford Prefect. Mums met in the park and exchanged gossip about their families. They compared notes about their babies' teething problems. They also made sure that their friends knew that their little one had said his first words and taken his first steps weeks before any other child in the street. The old men smiled. They had heard it all before.

Right: The helter skelter is on what became Moor Lane bus station. The funfair, at the corner of Blackhorse Street and Ashburner Street, was in full swing on New Year's Eve 1956. The little sideshows attracted young men trying to impress their girlfriends with their ability to hit three separate playing cards with their darts. Fans of John Wayne films tried their luck with a rifle as metal ducks passed by on a rail. There were candy floss, ice cream and toffee apples. Best of all were the baked potatoes and hot chestnuts to keep out the winter chill. A little tot walked by, clutching a plastic bag that contained a goldfish. It was destined for a bowl on top of the sideboard. The family cat waited at home, licking its lips in anticipation. The roundabouts, with their gaily decorated horses, were hand operated. The coconut mats on which we slid down the helter skelter tickled our legs. Cheeky lads stood at the bottom and wolf whistled as the girls showed their legs on the way down. The fair had been held here since 1929, moving from its former site in Victoria Square. In the background the gas works on Gas Street loomed large on the skyline. In the foreground the driver of the horse and cart whistled the introduction to 'Singing the blues', a big hit at the time for Guy Mitchell and Tommy Steele.

Below: There was an early spring nip in the air in Moss Bank Park. The trees were still waiting to burst into their full glory. At the moment they looked a little forlorn. Despite the chilly weather, walkers were out and about in large numbers. The reddened cheeks of the bonny baby on the right showed that it was not the best of days for open topped carriages. His proud young dad sported a typical haircut favoured by young men in the late 50s. He had a slicked back quif. But he was definitely not a Teddy boy. His sideburns were too short. The father on the left, from an older generation, was taking no chances that his son would race off on his trike. It had a telescopic arm fitted to its boot so that the lad could be reeled in if he got too ambitious. There was no work today, so families could enjoy their time together. It was Good Friday, April 1958. Many people stuck to church traditions and abstained from eating meat. The fishmonger had done good business the day before. The start of the Easter weekend was also a chance to prepare for Sunday. After the church service children wolfed down their chocolate Easter eggs. They painted faces on hardboiled eggs. Some went off to find a slope and have a game of egg rolling.

On the home front

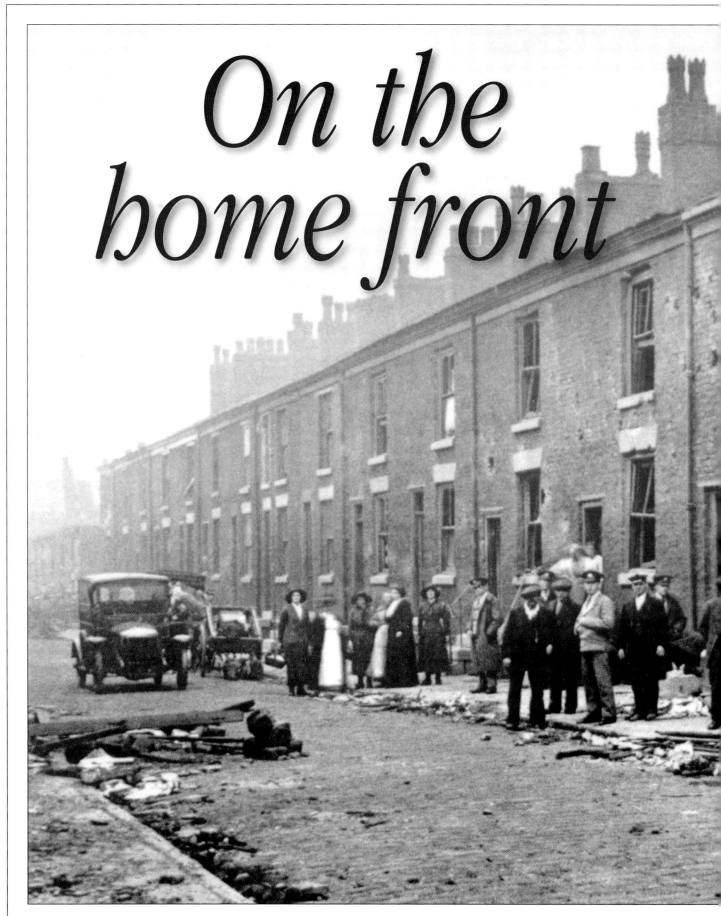

The east side of Kirk Street, looking towards Deane Road, has suffered from bomb damage during the war. That is obvious to anyone looking at the scene. It is only with closer examination that you come to realise that it was not a Heinkel or Junkers that caused the carnage. The men's caps and mufflers, the women's long skirts and the style of the car on the left give the game away. Bomb damage it certainly is, but this is an episode from 1916, during the first world war. Although aerial bombardment became commonplace during the Spanish Civil War and World War II, they were not the first conflicts in which air power was used. Ferdinand, Graf von Zeppelin flew his first airship in Germany in 1900. During the Great War this form of aircraft was used with some success on long range bombing raids. They could fly higher than the aeroplanes of the day. That gave them protection from attack in the air and kept them out of reach of fire from the ground. At the time many people thought that the airship was the future for both wartime and peacetime flight. However, spectacular disasters involving the R101 and the Hindenburg in the 1930s eroded public confidence in this form of air travel. Kirk Street residents did not offer an opinion on the subject. They were too stunned to be included amongst the casualties of war.

Above: A hot cuppa and a bite to eat helped a little. The refreshment being doled out from the emergency food van gave some comfort to those whose homes and lives had been shattered the day before. The blank, harrowed faces show that they were still in shock. No amount of information on the newsreels or civil defence practice sessions prepared them for the real thing. When it came it was with enormous power. On 12 October 1941 a ton of high explosive, dropped by a German bomber, cut a swathe through Punch Street and Ardwick Street. Even houses half a mile away felt the blast as windows disintegrated. There were 80 families made homeless by this single strike. Even worse, 11 people lost their lives and dozens more were injured. Many lost their entire possessions. They were left with just what they stood up in. Neighbours and relations rallied round, donating clothes and temporary furniture. But, belongings with a sentimental attachment, like family photographs, were irreplaceable. Civil defence groups, such as the WVS, provided shelter in church halls and schoolrooms. The food van was one of a fleet provided by the motor manufacturer Henry Ford, in conjunction with his son Edsel. Gordon's, a local firm, provided the support for its maintenance and running costs. Note the blinkers on the headlights, fitted as part of the blackout restrictions.

It was not just the major industrial cities that suffered from the Luftwaffe's bombing raids in World War II. In October 1941 Punch Street, just off Deane Road, shared the pain of Manchester, Liverpool and the others. Stunned residents and onlookers viewed the scene of devastation. Bowler hatted council officials stood around discussing the situation. Civil defence members tried to do what they could. Workmen began the difficult task of clearing the rubble. Care had to be taken. Damaged brickwork might yet come crashing down on them. There might be unexploded bombs lying under the debris, just waiting to catch out the unwary. Already the death toll stood at 11, with 64 more injured here and on nearby Ardwick Street. Bolton could now share the misery felt night after night by Londoners as they took the brunt of the blitz that the enemy unleashed earlier in the year. Hitler had decided against an invasion of Britain. His fighter planes were unable to command the skies, having been beaten in the 1940 Battle of Britain. Instead he decided to bomb the country into submission. He did not reckon upon our determination to see it through, come what may. We succeeded, but it was not without a great deal of sacrifice of both lives and property. Many of those on Punch Street would have nightmares for years about the hail of death and destruction that rained down upon them that fateful autumn night.

Below: In August 1944 the war still had a year to run. Of course, we did not know that at the time. But, the signs were good. The Allies liberated Paris and the tricolor hung from the Eiffel Tower for the first time in four years. To the east the Russians were driving back the Germans in an advance on Warsaw. But, Hitler was not done for just yet. He retaliated by launching V-1 and V-2 rockets on the south of England. Britain needed to be ready for one last effort towards victory. That task was not just in the hands of our menfolk. Women had a huge part to play, just as they had throughout the war. Here a branch of the Women's Junior Air Corps is on parade. These young women, some of them little more than girls, were ready to play their part. Throughout World War II the supposedly weaker sex had stood firm in the face of adversity. They worked the land and ran the factories. They mobilised in civil defence units. Lady Reading's Women's Voluntary Service drove vans and ambulances into fire ravaged areas as bombs rained down around them. Red Cross and St John Ambulance members carried out similar functions. Nurses took care of those injured in battle, close to the front lines, with little regard for their own safety. WAAFs served on airfields that were strafed by German fighters. Women became the fighting force that Hitler forgot.

County Borough of Bolton.
'PILES' OF BOOKS CAMPAIGN
THIS IS THE SPOT.
LEAVE ALL YOUR OLD BOOKS
MAGAZINES IN GOOD HANDS.
The Sky is the Limit.
BUILD A MONUMENT TO HIT
REMEMBER;
EVERY 'PIECE' BRINGS NEARER 'PE

'Every piece brings nearer peace'. It was one of many slogans we had in the second world war. The message was clear. Each book, newspaper or scrap of paper could be recycled as part of the war effort. Posters on hoardings and large billboards told us to 'Be like dad, keep mum' and to be aware that 'Careless talk costs lives' in an effort to prevent enemy spies learning our secrets. 'Make do and mend' urged us to conserve clothing. 'Dig for victory' encouraged the nation to turn gardens, parks and waste land into allotments. 'Do the job he left behind' and 'Come into our factories' were messages to women to play their part. But the biggest efforts centred on acquiring raw materials that were in short supply. Our merchant ships were harassed by German U-boat packs. Supplies reaching our shores were strictly limited. We had to use what we had at home. Salvage drives became part and parcel of our daily lives. In this photograph it was paper that was being collected. Prized novels and magazines were donated as we all made sacrifices in the struggle with Hitler. At other times there were aeroplane, warship or tank weeks. Then we surrendered our old saucepans, front door knockers, railings and brass bedsteads. They reappeared months later as Spitfires, destroyers or armoured vehicles.

Warburtons - 125 years and still growing

I t was two brothers, George and Thomas Warburton who began the story back in 1876 when George agreed to back his brother's ambition to own a small grocery shop at 125 Blackburn Road. From these humble beginnings - and Ellen Warburton's now famed loaves and flour cakes - the business took root.

George's son Henry joined the bakery business aged just 16. He was an intelligent and ambitious young man with an eye for an opportunity. Under the guidance of his father and uncle Thomas, Henry learnt quickly and by the age of 25, was a Master Baker and completely in charge at Warburtons. He was to prove a real and dynamic driving force behind the company's success.

State-of-the-art machinery and new double decker ovens drove the business forward. However, Henry never once took his eye off product quality and personally supervised all aspects of production.

Between the late 1880s and 1915 Henry continued to expand Warburtons, moving bakeries four times in 25 years and finishing with the opening of Back o'the Bank in 1915. Despite the First World War and its effects on manpower and resources, Henry worked on to complete his Model Bakery that was officially opened by Rachel Warburton on July 14 that year.

With prosperity came influence in the community as Henry began to trade in local property and stood as a

Liberal candidate - the beginning of a 36-year history of public service.

The 30s marked two momentous events in the company's development. Henry Warburton died on 5th September 1936 and the subsequent year saw the arrival of the Simplex Continuous Oven which was credited with helping the business survive its toughest trading period to date - the 30s. Henry's three sons now took over the reins. George, Harry and Billy decided to invest in more equipment in order to survive and thrive and were to soon to boast the most modern bakery in Lancashire.

Right: Rachel Warburton and children outside the shop in Blackburn Road.
Below: The Warburtons family outside the bakery with the delivery vans and drivers.

With the arrival of the fourth generation during the late 1940s, Warburton's appetite for expansion and development continued. The family had always believed that quality bread depended on having the very best, the best flour, equipment and ovens. In the 50s there was a realisation that a strong team of good people to help the family build the business was also a vital ingredient. The decade saw senior personnel from outside the

family joining the business, aside from Jim Aldred, the company secretary since 1936, who had been a close colleague of Harry and Billy.

Above: A shopper in the 1950s buying her Eatmore Malt loaf at the corner shop. It was a favourite of many households from the 1930s until the late 1950s

Left: Nellie Wallace the music hall star tasting the Eatmore Malt loaf in the 1930s, with Henry Warburton, his wife Rachel (left) and son George (right). **Below:** A family of bakers from 1876.

Warburtons grew through acquisition of several smaller companies in the North West, including Imperial Bakeries, manufacturers of Soreen Malt Loaf - still a market-leading brand today.

Between 1951 and 1965, Warburtons group bread sales doubled

through its five bakeries and 38 confectionery shops. During this time, in its pursuit of the best quality bread, Warburtons began to gain control over the flour quality from very reluctant millers. As Derrick Warburton remembers: During the 50s, the culture of making the best bread we could began to take hold and this has thankfully remained with us, perhaps now more than ever.

The company continued to thrive into the 70s, consolidating the great advances of the previous two decades,

burgeoning new product development programme to boost the long-standing successful lines has brought us to the beginning of the 21st century.

This year is a special year as 2001 marks the company's 125th anniversary.

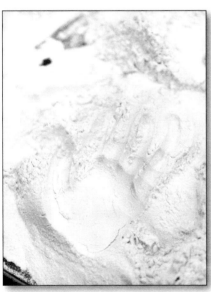

building new bakeries starting with Burnley. Market changes in the late 70s and 80s meant that the traditional corner shop trade was losing out to the massive growth of the supermarket. Warburtons had to adapt to a new market environment and with this came the realisation that the bread needed to be marketed, something which had never been formalised before this date.

The 1990s began with the fifth generation taking the reins and a consolidation of the business back to baking bread. Expansion followed with the building of new bakeries in Nottingham, Bellshill in Scotland and Wednesbury in the West Midlands. This, along with the

In the words of the current Chairman, Jonathan Warburton: I am quite sure that when Ellen and Thomas baked their first loaves back in 1876, their greatest hope would be that this new product development could help them further establish their grocery shop in Bolton. I just wonder what they would think now as we move into our 125th year as a family business.

Top left: Investment in new technology and state-of-the-art equipment is a vital part of Warburtons success. *Above right: Warburtons 550 vehicles deliver supplies of fresh bread across the trading regions to 6000 customers every week. Left: Warburtons celebrating its 125th anniversary in 2001 and still growing... Right: Jonathan Warburton, the newly-appointed Chairman of Warburtons.*

Sporting life

King George V cut a fine and manly figure as he was presented to the teams before the 1926 Cup Final at Wembley. It was an all Lancashire final. Bolton Wanderers beat Manchester City in a game settled by a single goal, inevitably scored by David Jack. He had scored the first ever Wembley Cup Final goal three years earlier when he helped Bolton lift the trophy in front of a crowd of nearly 200,000, most of them having gate crashed. It was the final when the policeman on a white horse helped restore order. Bolton went on to win the Cup for a third time in the 1920s, beating Portsmouth in 1929. David Jack missed that game. He had been sold for a record £10,750 to Arsenal in 1928. Fans accused the board of selling their top player in order to finance a new stand. Waiting patiently at the end of the line on 24 April 1926 was Bolton's goalkeeper, RH 'Dick' Pym. He played in all three of the side's Wembley triumphs. A Devonian fisherman, he played for Exeter City before the first world war. He served in the Army as a PTI sergeant in the Devonshire Regiment. Later, he transferred to the East Surrey Regiment, with whom he was wounded in action. Bolton Wanderers paid £5,000 in 1921 for his transfer, then a record for a goalkeeper. Pym did not concede a goal in any of his three finals and went on to play three times for England. He retired in 1930 and returned to fishing. Dick Pym died in 1988 at the ripe old age of 95.

Disasters at football stadiums have plagued our enjoyment on too many occasions. There was the horror of Ibrox, during an 'old firm' match in 1971, when 66 died. In 1985 the Bradford fire killed 50 spectators and the riot at the Belgian Heysel Stadium left 41 dead. In 1989 the crush at Hillsborough killed 96 fans and paved the way for the Taylor report on soccer safety. It was nearly half a century too late for 33 of the spectators on the Embankment at Burnden Park. On 9 March 1946 there were supposed to be about 69,000 in the ground watching the FA Cup tie against Stoke City. The interest in the game prompted thousands more than the official attendance to gain entry by one means or another. This helped to cause the crush that made it the blackest day in Bolton Wanderers' history. The police had closed the gates an hour before the incident. The surging crowd outside broke through the police ranks and knocked down fences to get into the already packed enclosure. When the steel barriers on the terraces collapsed under the weight of the swell people were pushed to the ground and were trampled or suffocated. St John Ambulance workers, police and volunteers struggled to help, but it was all to no avail for those who were beyond help. The Home Secretary, Chuter Ede, ordered an inquiry. It achieved little.

Bottom: Salford artist LS Lowry used Bolton Wanderers soccer supporters as the subject of one of his most famous works. 'Going to the match' is now owned by the Professional Footballers' Association. It shows fans on their way to Burnden Park. They were moving along just such a street as Viking Street. On match day the street would be filled with cars between 2 pm and 5 pm on alternate Saturdays. This was well before satellite TV ruled football and decided that games should kick off whenever the television moguls decided. Viking Street echoed to then sound of rattles being cranked by excited children. Local youngsters offered their services as little security guards. 'Mind your car, mister?' It was worth a threepenny bit to avoid some urchin scratching the paintwork. Some of us came to the game on our bikes. We parked them in a Viking Street back yard and gave the householder a few pennies for the privilege. In the 1950s the Wanderers were a major force to be reckoned with. Injuries, that old Wembley hoodoo, had robbed them of victory in the 1953 cup final. There was not long to wait for success. In 1958, a few months after this photograph was taken, they beat Manchester United 2-0 to lift the Cup. Fans cheered as Nat Lofthouse put the ball and Harry Gregg, United's keeper, into the back of the net. It is rumoured that the following month Nat met Harry on Viking Street. Nat nodded a greeting to him and Gregg promptly threw himself into the gutter.

Below: This was 1966. It was the year that England last won something at soccer. It is also the only year that the national team won something! But, this is not Wembley where Geoff Hurst was banging in his hat trick against the Germans. This stadium is Burnden Park, the former pride and joy of Bolton Wanderers. The ground was held in such high esteem that the Football Association used it as a venue for many important matches. The terraces were filled with 'foreigners' from Manchester United, Everton and other major teams playing

FA Cup semi finals here. But to Trotters' fans it was the place of worship that they came to on alternate Saturdays. For over a century they made their way through the turnstiles. Little lads were given a lift over or squashed into the same stile as dad. Meat pies were washed down by cups of steaming hot Bovril. Children munched on Nuttall's Mintoes. Sweet sellers paraded around the edge of the field. Money was passed down to them and they threw a bag of toffees to the purchaser standing 20 rows back. They were as accurate as a

Dougie Holden pass. The club began life as Christ Church soccer team in 1874. It played at Pikes Lane, becoming Bolton Wanderers in 1877. Bolton joined the Football League in 1888 as one of its founder members. The popularity of the side meant it had to move to a bigger ground and Burnden Park became its home in 1895. The highest official attendance was recorded in 1933 when 69,912 watched a game against Manchester City. The Wanderers left Burnden Park in 1997 for the Reebok Stadium.

Events & Occasions

The Earl of Derby cut a fine figure in Victoria Square on the day the Civic Centre was officially opened. His handsome walking cane, morning dress and gleaming top hat marked him out as an aristocrat of distinction. The Square was packed with people from all walks of life. Local councillors and law officers put on their robes and chains of office in honour of the occasion. More humble townspeople lined the pavements to share in the glory of the day. Some of them popped into the Grapes after the ceremony; something they continued to do until 1960. Then the hotel was demolished as part of the town's redevelopment plans. Successive Earls of Derby had longstanding links with the town. The manor lands and estates around Bolton belonged to various families after the Norman Conquest, but most of them held the position of Earl of Derby. One title holder, William de Ferrers, granted the charter of 1253 that made Bolton a market town and borough. James Stanley, the 7th Earl, died in the town. He was very active during the English Civil War. Stanley was chosen by Charles II to command the forces of Cheshire and Lancashire in the proposed Royalist rising. On 15 August 1651 he landed at Wyre Water, but was totally defeated at Wigan, being severely wounded and escaping with difficulty. He was later captured near Nantwich and sentenced to death. James Stanley then met a sticky end. He was brought to Bolton and beheaded in Churchgate on 15 October 1651.

You could hardly see the town hall steps on Tuesday, 20 June 1939. They were taken up by scores of specially invited guests and dignitaries. Gathered to greet the Earl of Derby, they were aware of the historic traditions of his family. The 14th Earl, Edward Stanley, served three terms as prime minister in the 1850s and 1860s. When the latest in the line came to open the Civic Centre he was fulfilling the dream of Lord Leverhulme. He had proposed the redevelopment of the town in the early 1900s. Bolton Council amended his plans and extended the 1873 Town Hall. Building of the Civic Centre began in 1931 on what is now known as Le Mans Crescent, named after the French town that was Bolton's first twin town. Slums around Howell Croft and Spring Gardens were cleared. The Sessions and Police Department opened in October 1934 and the Public Health offices and Library in 1938. The opening of the Museum was delayed until after the war. As Lord Derby's car drove towards the ceremonial gathering a family tradition was observed. Blinds were drawn across the passenger windows as it passed Churchgate. The Stanley family did not wish to look at the spot where the 7th Earl's head was separated from its shoulders.

The ceremonial opening of the new civic centre buildings in 1938 was a very special day in the town's history. It was marked by the attendance of the highest in the land. Queen Elizabeth posed next to Lord Derby in Victoria Square. She had been thrust into the limelight less than two years earlier. Her husband Albert, Duke of York, found himself taking over the British throne as King George VI. His brother, Edward VIII, had abdicated in the face of the scandal surrounding his relationship with the American socialite, Wallis Simpson. The new king did not relish life in the glare of the spotlight. Luckily, he had a strong willed wife who would support him throughout his reign. She was popular with the public

as she broke the mould of foreign royals becoming the consorts of our monarchs. Her presence in Bolton made sure that the occasion made the headlines in the national press. Mayor Halstead beamed with pleasure, knowing the project had at last come to fruition. Behind the scenes many others were grateful for the opportunity the development had given them. For about eight years the building work had lifted the spectre of unemployment for local workmen. About 800 of them had escaped the dark days of the depression years that blighted so many others. They were thankful they did not have to share the hardship that caused the men from Jarrow to march on London in 1936.

It would not do to wear all those furs today. The animal rights groups would go berserk. Perhaps the woman looking over her shoulder was an early member of the movement. She seems far from impressed with the visitor to the cotton mill. She has a look of Kathy Staff, the actress famous for Norah Batty in TV's 'Last of the summer wine'. Perhaps she is some distant relative, but that cannot be pursued without checking for wrinkled stockings! Whoever she was Queen Elizabeth, wife of King George VI, had interrupted her work. Born Elizabeth Bowes Lyon in 1900, she became one of the most popular members of the Royal family. She and her husband were respected for not fleeing the country during the war. When Buckingham Palace was bombed she said that she then knew something of how London's Eastenders felt. By the time she reached her own 100th birthday in the first year of the 21st century she had become revered as the 'Queen Mum'. Her visit in 1948 was at a time when the cotton industry was about to fall into terminal decline. As the 20th century began there were 200 mills, sheds and associated industries providing employment for 58,000. By the time that Queen Elizabeth came to call only half that number drew a wage packet from cotton.

Above: Mums put on their pinnies and slaved away in the kitchen. By the time they had finished they had enough to make the tables laid out in Furness Avenue, Tonge Moor groan under the weight of the goodies. Just to add a touch of class, pretty floral decorations set off the feast delightfully. The scene was repeated in every street across the nation. The children sat patiently, waiting for the command to tuck in. They demolished the lot in 10 minutes flat. There had been few occasions for celebration in their short lives, so they made the most of this one. This was in August 1945. In May they had rejoiced that the war in Europe had ended. News had come through that now the war with Japan was done. Emperor Hirohito surrendered after the B-29 bomber Enola Gay dropped an atom bomb on Hiroshima and Nagasaki was similarly attacked three days later. It was with mixed emotions that the adults celebrated. There was joy that the war years were over. There was relief that no more sacrifices had to be made. But it was all tinged with sadness. Every person on Furness Avenue had a relative or friend who had lost someone on a foreign field. Those attending this party were exclusively women and children. The men were away, working for the war effort or still in the armed forces. Not all made it back.

Above right: The adverts around the shop on the left were simple and to the point. A happy, smiling face suggested that we drink Lyons' Green Label tea. The one recommending

Horniman's tea countered it. That brand offered gifts as well as a tasty beverage. Craven A was the cigarette being promoted. It was one of the few to introduce a filter tip. Until then smokers risked removing a layer of skin from their lips if they took a fag out of their mouths too quickly. Craven A had a slogan that would make modern health

conscious folk wince. As the tip was supposed to cool the smoke it was suggested that you 'smoke them for your throat's sake'. There was not a great deal of activity inside this shop on Bow Street on 8 July 1938. Its windows had been blown out, along with those of some neighbouring properties. The culprit was an acetylene cylinder that had exploded. Workmen had been busy constructing the Croal sewer when the accident occurred. One man was killed. The people in the crowd that gathered to watch the repairs did not worry about brands of tea being advertised. They cared little for cigarettes, untipped or otherwise. Their thoughts were with the family of the poor chap who perished.

Victoria Square was awash with a sea of faces in May 1945. The announcement of the victory in Europe was made from the town hall steps. Forever, this would be known as VE Day. On 7 May peace came to a battered Europe in a small red schoolhouse in Rheims. The German chief of staff signed the unconditional surrender under the watchful gaze of General Eisenhower, the Allied Supreme commander. The following day, Britain took to the streets. Bolton was one of hundreds of towns and cities where the inhabitants stood close to a first world war memorial and listened to the official proclamation of peace. Their joy that the end had

come was tempered by the knowledge that so many would not be coming home to share their happiness. The words on the memorial said it all. 'In undying memory of the men and women who gave their lives in the Great War.' Those same sentiments could now be applied to this war. Across the country stonemasons added the names of those who had fallen to the long list of those who made the ultimate sacrifice in 1914-18. As they made their way home, the crowds remembered that there was still a war in the east to be won. The Japanese were still engaging the Allies. That conflict continued for another three months, concluding with the atomic bomb attacks on Hiroshima and Nagasaki.

Above: The Queen's visit to Bolton in 1954 was a great time for us to show the flag. The crowd, mainly made up of mums and children, waved little flags on sticks as the cavalcade of royal cars bowled along the streets. The royal train brought its special passengers to Trinity Street. They walked the red carpet and stepped into the limousines that took them along Bradshawgate, Great Moor Street and into Newport Street, before alighting in Victoria Square. Children, many dressed in their Brownie or Cub uniforms, cheered wildly. Mums hung onto their headscarves as the noise reached a crescendo. The monarchy had seldom been so popular. How many of those little girls, in their short ankle socks, or lads showing shiny knees can ever forget the day when they first saw the Queen in real life? Now parents and grandparents themselves, they can still recall the magic of the moment. A lot of them had been waiting patiently for hours for just a brief sighting of her.

Yet, it was worth it. They could go home and look at the coronation mugs they had been given at school two years before. On every one of those mementoes a picture of Queen Elizabeth gazed out at them. After today the children were convinced that she had waved especially at them. That would stay with them forever.

Below: It may have dawned damp and cloudy on 22 October 1954, but Bolton folk did not let the weather depress their spirits. They turned out in their thousands to line the roads leading to Hotel Street, at the corner of Victoria Square. It was the day after Trafalgar Day and we had a sense of history and a vision for the future in those days. As she passed Naisby's, the draper and gents' outfitter established before Queen Victoria was on the throne, Queen Elizabeth II turned to inspect the guard of honour. It was a proud day for the servicemen, many of whom wore medals bravely won in the second world war. The Queen was honouring the town with a special visit. It was only right that her subjects showed their support. She was on a royal tour of Lancashire, accompanied by her husband, the Duke of Edinburgh. It was now about 10 am and many of us had been there since just after dawn, so anxious were we to get a good spot. Most of us had glimpsed pictures of our monarch on flickering black and white TV sets when her coronation was broadcast the year before. But, this was an opportunity to see her in the flesh. It was not one to be spurned. Elizabeth was still a young woman. She had acceded to the throne in 1952 at the tender age of 25 and served us well throughout the remainder of the century and beyond.

The rain pitter pattered from the skies. It glistened on the cobbled setts, but no one bothered. The Queen's 1954 visit was too important an occasion to be dampened by a little wet weather. She inspected the guard of honour formed by members of the Royal North Lancashire regiment. Queen Elizabeth II looked keenly at the medals the men wore so proudly. The older soldiers had seen action and served king, queen and country with gallantry. The officer escorting Her Majesty cast his eyes down to the men's boots. Even if they were spotted with rain there was no excuse for them not to gleam brightly. The young queen, looking very neat and trim in her sober outfit, had only come to the throne two years earlier. She had been in Kenya when news of the death of her father, George VI, came through. It was a shock to the nation. He had been ill for some time, but the end came all too soon. He was only 56. Elizabeth rose to the challenge with a maturity that belied her tender years. During her reign she continued to show the same calm and poise she displayed on that rainy day in Bolton. Despite the questionable behaviour of some of her family, Elizabeth II stayed a cut above. We loved her all the more for it.

On the move

The horse pulling the laundry cart takes a disdainful look at the tram making its way into town along Chorley New Road. This is one of the vehicles that helped make true horsepower redundant. For hundreds of years these handsome creatures had met our transport needs. Yet, within a few short decades, steam, oil and electricity consigned them to history. No wonder the poor thing wore blinkers. He would have wanted to have all those developments kept out of his sight. Some comfort could have been taken in knowing that the life of the tram was sorely limited. Even in 1929, when this N tram was moving smoothly along its tracks, the beginning of its end was under way. By the time Judy Garland sang 'Clang, clang went the trolley' in her 1944 film 'Meet me in St Louis', the day of the tram in Bolton was largely done. At its peak the tram system supported 158 cars in the 1920s. It had seen off competition from steam omnibuses that ran in Edwardian times to Darcy Lever and Brownlow Fold. But the assault from motor buses was too much. Single decker Leylands were introduced in 1923. With the coming of trolley buses in the 1930s, the writing was on the wall. They took over some of the tram routes, particularly on the run to Leigh. Trolley buses were themselves phased out in 1958 as large 30 foot double decker buses were brought in.

It may have been back in the 1930s but there was a chance of modern road rage breaking out on Bank Street. The tram and car seem to be on collision course. It seems futile because the tram has no alternative. It is stuck to its tracks. Surely the car driver will move aside. He must have been well used to seeing the tramcars on the streets of Bolton. They had been there since 1880 when the first horse drawn ones appeared. Teams of four or five noble steeds strained as they pulled the heavy cars and their passenger loads. Electrification at the turn of the century made life easier for the horses who took happily to their retirement. The new trams could also cater for larger loads. The first electric ones carried 44 passengers, split evenly between the two decks. This tramcar was on its way to Tonge Moor, as shown by the letter T on its front. Each route had its own letter, usually referring to the first letter of its destination. On this day the only person making real headway was the workman barrowing his tools to his next job. The driver of Pratts' lorry was not impressed. He had worked hard enough turning the engine over to get it started. The starting handle below the radiator took some cranking.

The journey to Tonge Moor was usually sedate and unremarkable. But something went wrong on this day in August 1939. The tram had left the tracks and jammed itself against the side of Bow Street. Fortunately the accident was not as bad as one two years later when 31 were hurt in a bad smash on Folds Road. Even so, passengers had a nasty shock when the tramcar slid sideways down the street. Taking a corner too quickly was the usual cause of such incidents. Trams were first operated by Edmund Holden and Company. His horse drawn cars ran on tracks to Moses Gate, Dunscar and Halliwell. Bolton Corporation bought out his lease in 1899. It inherited 350 horses and 48 trams. The animals were soon made redundant as tracks were relaid, ready for the gradual introduction of electric trams in the first few years of the 20th century. Route letters, rather than numbers, were used from 1902. This one ought to have been rescheduled as route N, as it was going nowhere! The accident soon attracted an interested crowd of onlookers. It is part of the makeup of all of us that we have this fascination for disaster. Any crash on a motorway produces a tail back on the opposite carriageway as drivers rubberneck for a better view.

Above: Driving a tram was a damp and draughty occupation. The passengers might be cosy inside, but pity the poor chap in charge on the platform of the G service to Walkden. He should have qualified for danger money in our wet and windy Lancashire climate. Open to the elements, he was fortunate to find that this November day in 1944 had dawned bright. His tram was the last to make this journey. The service, along with many others, was being phased out. Within a few short years all trams had run their final journeys. It is ironic that they have made a comeback in recent years as councils have tried to find a solution to city centre congestion. Leeds, Sheffield, Manchester and Newcastle have all decided that some of the old ways were best, after all. The little hairdresser's shop on the right belongs to an age when there was no such thing as unisex. Barbers gave men a short back and sides, plus a dab of Brylcreem on top. There might have been a purchase of a packet of razor blades and 'something for the weekend', but that was all. It was the ladies who went to hairdressing parlours. All that crimping, perming and dyeing was not for a red blooded male. Not only that, but the women would have thrown him out of the shop had he tried to get in.

Below left: Not a parking ticket, pay booth or barrier in sight. This is how to encourage people to come into town. Unfortunately, the car is now seen as a disadvantage on our town and city centre streets. Its petrol is taxed to the hilt and its parking fees fixed so high that it hurts. Moor Lane bus station once happily shared this site with the private motorist. In the rows of vehicles parked there try to spot a foreign make. It will take quite a while before you can cry 'Snap!'. The Union Foundry of Rothwell and Hick once had its home here. It was the first engineering works in the town. Bessemers Ltd produced steel here. The company owed its development to the Hertfordshire inventor and engineer, Henry Bessemer (1813-98). He had perfected a process whereby blowing air through melted cast iron not only purified it but also heated it further. This allowed the purified iron to be easily poured into steel ingots. The site was cleared in 1927 and the bus station opened in 1930. Some of the car drivers had parked up to make a visit to the Odeon cinema. At the peak of movie popularity there were 22 cinemas in Bolton. Gradually they dwindled into oblivion. Television, bingo and videos took their progressive toll.

Bottom: Folds Road, at its junction with Kay Street and Bank Street, is often choked with traffic. The authorities must have thought that it was likely to be so even over half a century ago. Why else would there have been a bobby on point duty?

Yet, in 1950, he did not seem to have much to do. He was offering a personal service to the solitary van crossing the old tram tracks. They were a reminder of the days when clanking cars carried passengers into town. Now they were no more. Only the rails remained. The public now used single decker buses, like the one disappearing into the distance. They relied heavily on them. Petrol rationing was still in force. Money was tight. The private motoring boom was still the best part of a decade away. For the policeman it was a quiet job. His busy days on traffic control lay ahead of him. When the roads got busier those white sleeves would earn their corn. Arms like ramrods would be held aloft, out to the side or bent from the elbow, all indicating clearly whose turn it was to move on. The Highway Code even had a section on hand signals that the police used when on point duty. You ignored them at your peril.

In the summer of 1951 the trolley bus to Leigh was about to leave the bus station at Howell Croft South. The route was one that had been taken over from the tram service before the war. These were the days of conductors and their female counterparts, the clippies. They handed out tickets produced from a paper roll within a hand cranked ticket machine. Children used to play games with the numbers on the tickets. They added up the digits and came up with a number that translated into 'I love Johnny Brown', 'I am an elephant' or some other silly message that had them rolling in the aisles. Every so often an inspector would get on board to make sure we had not ridden past our stop. He was also there to check the efficiency of the service and the work of the driver and his conductor. This was the inspiration for the hugely successful TV series 'On the buses', starring Reg Varney. Stephen Lewis made a name for himself as the glum, long suffering inspector. At the time of this photograph the word 'sitcom' was some way ahead. Few of us owned a television. Those who did had only one channel to watch. The rest of us listened to the radio, amused by Tommy Handley in 'ITMA' and entertained by the daily happenings at Ambridge in 'The Archers'.

Above: Deane Road had its own form of dual carriageway in April 1953. The oil drums and little signalman's lamps performed as good a job as any set of bollards and concrete verges. The shiny chrome and gleaming coachwork on the cars tell us that these motorists took a real pride in their machines. It took hours of elbow grease, not to mention turtle wax and Duraglit. The health and safety brigade would have fun today with the sharp bumpers and protruding AA and RAC badges. The little sidelights, mounted on the wing, would have caught its eye as well. Many vehicles had small semaphore arms mounted on their sides. These popped out when the driver wanted to indicate he was about to turn. Drivers also used hand signals to show their intentions. The one in front of the lorry belonging to Sheldon and Co was about to turn right. If it had been a left turn his arm would have been moved in a circular fashion. Hand signals used to be a necessary part of the driving test. The lorry was approaching 2 Deane Road. This property was the Woodman's Cottage pub, a beerhouse owned by the Openshaw Brewery of West Gorton, Manchester. It closed in 1959. The site now lies in between Moor Lane fire station and a car parking area.

Right: The ordinary passenger train on the far platform had come from Manchester Exchange, but the one on the left carried a special group of travellers. We all have our hobbies, some of them amuse others, especially when that hobby becomes an obsession. Lovers of the railways often fall into such a category, mocked by many as 'anoraks', they really could not care less. They are too wrapped up in their subject. Members of the grandly titled Railway Correspondence and Travel Society were on Great Moor Street Station on 26 July 1953. They had chartered a special train for the day and spent it examining locos, wheel arrangements, stations, marshalling yards and signal boxes. It was a day of sheer bliss for these enthusiasts. As little lads they stood on draughty platforms and hung over the parapets of bridges in all weathers, filling exercise books with train numbers. They collected used tickets and cigarette cards of famous locomotives. These they pasted lovingly into scrapbooks. Some of them are now collectors' items at antique fairs. They are more than just collections from the age of steam. Hidden beneath the exhibits are the memories and nostalgia for those days of steam. The piercing shrill of the whistle, the puff of the plume of white smoke and the clank of the wheels across the points are contained in those album pages, unseen, but there all the same.

Below: The chap on the right crouched down to examine every nook and cranny of the station and track. Special trains were run for railway enthusiasts, so popular was the pastime. The tank engine in view was a 2-4-2 arrangement, of a type first built in Horwich in 1889. The famous Loco Works provided rolling stock for Bolton, Britain and the rest of the world. It built its last steam locomotive in 1957. The works continued with the formation of British Rail Workshops Division in 1963. Horwich then became a wagon repair works. Plans for the rail network had been first mooted in 1822. The reasons were twofold. Firstly, it was decided to break the stranglehold the canal owners had upon the transportation of goods. The second reason was probably more important. Canals had served industry well, but they could not cope with the increasing volume of merchandise being produced. The Bolton to Leigh railway started at Great Lever, near to the Bolton-Bury-Manchester canal. Its terminus was near the Leeds-Liverpool canal. The line was the first steam operated railway in the northwest. The enthusiasts knew all this history as they examined for themselves the gas lighting of the antique signal box. The taller structure above it is an old wagon hoist. The ghosts of famous old locomotives, Salamander and Veteran, built by Crook and Dean at the Phoenix Foundry, thundered through the station as the railway buffs enjoyed their day.

Shopping spree

By December 1946 the country was close to completing its first full year of peace since 1938. It would be some years yet until the nation was back on its feet. The cost of the war still bit hard. Rationing would continue into the 1950s. There were few cars on the roads. Petrol was in short supply and car ownership was still the province of the middle classes. Ordinary folk used public transport, like the Tonge Moor tram making its way along Bradshawgate, away from the cobbled Nelson Square. The trams were given letters, rather than numbers, to identify their route. This one sported the letter 'T'. Despite the hard times, children could always look on the bright side. A little group has become engrossed with the motorbike parked at the kerbside. They did not dwell on the past,

but looked forward to the time when they could bowl along the road astride a Norton or BSA. Further up the pavement, two other children were making their way home from school. They carried their satchels on their backs. These contained all that the budding scholar needed. Homework exercise books, backed in brown paper, carefully sharpened Lakeland pencils for colouring maps and a bottle of Quink to refill the fountain pen were carefully stored inside. Drawing compasses and a protractor were necessary tools to help with that knotty theorem in geometry. Then there was the 12 inch ruler. It was not just used for measuring, but for underlining your work. Teachers insisted that everything be neatly ruled off. We never asked why. It was just one of life's little mysteries.

Deansgate is one of Bolton's oldest roads. 'Gate' means road and this thoroughfare was the way out to Dene Valley and Deane Moor. Dene is old English for a valley. The spelling of names derived from this has varied over the ages. During the English Civil War Bolton was a hotbed of Puritanism, loyal to Cromwell. The town was attacked by Royalist troops in May 1644 and Deansgate was the scene of some of the heaviest fighting. Some 1,500 died in what became known as the Bolton Massacre. By late Victorian times there were other fights taking place, but this was nothing to do with civil unrest. There were over 20 pubs on Deansgate and demon drink turned it into what was politely called a 'lively place'. By the end of the 20th century the number had shrunk to just six and the atmosphere had undergone a great change. As the last century unfolded Deansgate grew in importance as a shopping area. This elevated view shows how busy it became. People dodged the increasing volume of traffic as they flooded the area. Shoppers had plenty of variety from which to choose. They walked the pavements under dozens of awnings of retail outlets that sold everything from furniture to foodstuffs. It is now home to many of our major stores, as well as banks and financial institutions.

The crowded pavements of Deansgate, close to its junction with Knowsley Street, offer a reminder of fashions from over 50 years ago. Young lads did not go into long trousers until they were well into double figures. That practice continued for many years. Most primary schools insisted on short trousers being worn until the 1970s, with a few holding out even later. Many men started to sport trilbies as they tried to throw off the working class connection with the flat cap. Women's skirt and coat lengths began to drift downwards once more. They had been higher during the war because material was in short supply. Women insisted on going out with their heads covered. It was regarded as slightly immodest or unladylike to be bare headed. The headscarf became the uniform of the age. It also provided a handy protection for the perm underneath. However those who went out with their curlers still in rather let the side down. This scene was pictured in December 1949. Christmas shopping was in full swing. Ration coupons had been hoarded and could now be blown on some fripperies for the festive season. There might be some nuts and an orange or two for the kiddies' stockings. A visit to Santa's grotto would be part of the day's treats. Parents paid their coppers and the children got the chance to sit on the old man's knee. Girls got a magic colouring book. It would get very soggy as they painted the picture with water that miraculously turned into paint. He gave the boys a toy trumpet. That was a popular choice with mums and dads at four o'clock on Christmas morning!

Below: The war memorial is about all that remains of the structures seen in this 1950s' photograph of Victoria Square. Singer's sewing machine shop was very popular in the immediate postwar years. Housewives treadled away making their own clothes and curtains. Money was tight. It made economic sense to use skills passed down from mother to daughter. There was also a sense of pride in drawing the curtains you had made or wearing a frock run up in your own front room. Girls stood still in front of the mirror as mum, with a mouth full of pins, made adjustments to the tucks and darts she had carefully crafted. After the row was demolished Singer went to the Deansgate end of Bradshawgate. The Manchester Furniture Warehouse moved to the corner of Deansgate and King Street. Battersby's furnishers reopened in new premises on Newport Street and traded from there until its closure in 1973. The war memorial was unveiled in 1928, a rather late acknowledgement of the sacrifices made by those who fell in the Great War. Further inscriptions were added after World War II. The bronze figures that flank the memorial were positioned there in 1933. One group represents the struggle of mankind to exist in harmony. The second group symbolises peace and the sacrifices made to achieve it.

Bottom: There was hardly a soul to be seen on the northeast side of Victoria Square, nearly half a century ago. Contrast that with the throngs seen today on what is often called simply The Precinct. Now pedestrianised, it is one of the more pleasant results of the modern planner. The Victoria Rose, set in the Square, is an attractive reminder of the cotton trade with Africa and the old fountains that once flowed here. Some of the Rose's petals are made from granite recycled from the fountains or of African origin. Victoria Square is really an extension of Newport Street. It is the former market square. The market moved here from Churchgate in 1824. In Victorian times shoppers would have watched street entertainers. Jugglers, acrobats and fire eaters kept the crowds amused and hoped they would dig deep when the hat was passed round. A flavour of those days has returned to the Square. Now we have buskers, with their guitars, saxophones and violins as a backdrop to our shopping. There is even an annual Buskers' Ball for local talent to have its chance to impress. Not everything from yesteryear belonged to the good old days. This scene from the 1950s is quite drab in comparison to what you can see today.

Below: Mention Coronation Street and everyone thinks of the long running TV soap. But, all towns have had a cobbled street with such a name. Bolton is no exception. The woman making her way along the cracked pavements of our Coronation Street was coming from Ashburner Street. She was passing the site of the old market. The street was once known as Back Newport Street, as it ran behind and parallel to Newport Street. It was renamed in 1838, in honour of Queen Victoria's coronation. A fire station, with its steam powered fire engines, once stood here. Pictured in 1957 it was now home to Hesford's and Ellison's, rivals in the sale of carpets and linoleum. The day of wall to wall carpeting in our houses was yet to come. The best room was carpeted, but lino, that hardwearing product of oxidised linseed oil, was to be found on the floor of many of the other rooms. We did not have money to burn on such extravagances as Wilton and Axminster all over the place. The shops moved to Great Moor Street soon after this photograph was taken, when the western side of Newport Street was demolished. The name of Coronation Street is now just a memory. It has become just an unnamed back alley.

The proprietor of the shop selling raincoats on the left hand side of Newport Street in December 1955 must have been rubbing his hands with glee. The weather was foul. Streetlights and those from the shop windows were reflected on the damp pavements leading from the south part of the street, across the junction with Great Moor Street and towards the town hall in the distance. At the crossroads there was a sign exhorting you to buy UCP tripe, that meal of stomach tissue soaked in vinegar that you either love or loathe. A diet that includes tripe, black pudding and pigs' trotters may seem strange to some. But, the Scots have sheep offal and suet in a haggis. The French pack the inner bits of a pig into their andouille sausage. So, where's the problem with our specialities? On its way towards the crossroads the no 23 bus, across the road from the Army recruiting office, sported an advert for winter grade Esso. ITV had just been born and viewers started to get used to the slogans and gimmicks employed by advertisers. In later years everyone knew the catchy ones used by the major oil companies. Esso had 'A tiger in the tank' to rival one of its main competitors who urged you to 'Keep going well, keep going Shell'.

Above: In 1957 this part of Newport Street, from Ashburner Street, past Exchange Street to Victoria Square, boasted a variety of busy, thriving little shops. Housewives enjoyed Boardman's special sausages. What was better than the breakfast time scene of sizzling bangers in the frying pan?

The women outside Morris's were checking the price of the shoes on sale. It seems strange to see a large sign advertising that the shop sold smart shoes. It would hardly tell anyone it sold the opposite! The shoppers' daughters would be more interested in tottering around on stiletto heels, but these wise women wanted what they termed 'sensible shoes'. Their offspring described them differently. 'Boring' was their description. Adamson's tobacconists was next door to the shoe shop. The full strength Capstan cigarettes on sale were only for the committed smoker, a drag on one of those when you got up in the morning was enough to send both your head and the room reeling. This set of shops, now demolished, was once nicknamed Shoe Alley and in earlier times known as Cheapside, the Octagon Theatre now occupies part of this site. Newport Street, from Victoria Square back to Great Moor Street, is pedestrianised today.

Above right: The view of the town hall, looking along Howell Croft North, was taken in the early 1960s. Betty's sweet store, next to the Civil Defence Social Club, was a treasure trove of good things that were bad for your teeth. Jelly babies, sherbet dips and licorice allsorts were too much of a temptation. The counter held the penny sweets, there were bootlaces, penny chews and love hearts. The shelves groaned under the weight of large glass bottles filled with pear drops, sherbet lemons and striped humbugs. The scales weighed out two ounces of sheer delight that were tipped into a little paper bag. Shoved into a warm pocket the sweets became sticky and mingled with the paper when we took them out to be scoffed. Two shillings' pocket money went a long way. We still had more than enough to buy the Dandy or Beano. The exploits of Denis the Menace, Korky the Cat and Lord Snooty kept us tickled pink. We chuckled over that doyen of Cactusville, Desperate Dan, as he munched his cow pies. As we got older we read about the immortal Wilson, Tupper of the Track and the finest soccer player known to anyone. If Limpalong Leslie could score a hat trick, so could we.

It is not surprising that traffic is restricted along Deansgate these days. Just look at the problems people had in 1957. Austin cars, babies in prams, Corporation buses and pedestrians criss crossed the carriageway. They all seemed to claim the right of passage. The clock outside Ellwood's Silks tells us that it was rush hour. Shoppers were off to an early flying start to the day. Office workers were making their way in for a day at their desks. There was little room for manoeuvre. The no 11 to Chorley passed its counterpart making the opposite journey. Double decker buses were a popular form of public transport in those days as car ownership was still not the norm. The top decks were well patronised. In addition to being able to smoke up there, passengers gained a new view of their locality. On their way into town fine views across the fields were offered. The congested streets meant that they had plenty of time to appreciate some of the fine architecture above the shop fronts. Those more interested in the day's events opened their newspapers. They read about the Russians launching Sputnik, the first man made satellite, into space. Marvellous, wasn't it? Man could send a craft hurtling around the earth at 18,000 miles an hour, but was unable to move a vehicle along Deansgate at much more than walking pace.

Above: You have to be of a certain age to recall a time when pavements had kerbs unsullied by yellow lines. There really were days when parking meters and traffic wardens did not exist. They had started to reach Bolton in 1965, but had not conquered Victoria Square just yet. Now, of course, you cannot even bring your car into the Precinct, much less park it. Locals probably grumbled about changes in the 1800s, just as we do today. At the start of the 19th century Victoria Square was just a pretty rural spot. There was a tinkling stream flowing through a pretty field and orchard. Close by a game of bowls was enjoyed on the green. Then, in 1820, it was decided to move the market here from Churchgate. That would not have gone down well with those who had taken pleasure in the serenity of the previous surroundings. From that date on Victoria Square, as it was later christened, became part of the commercial scene. The names on the shop fronts may have changed, but the activity continues just as before. At least, though, the shoppers in 1965 did not have to worry about the discarded rubbish from polystyrene trays of fast food that seem to litter our pavements all too often. Roadsweepers eventually clear those up, but the smell seems to linger forever.

Right: To take this photograph in 1963 the cameraman had probably just bought his film at Timothy White's chemist shop, as he was standing outside it at the Great Moor Street crossroads with Newport Street. The shop is now owned by Boot's. The pointed top of St Patrick's Church cast a shadow on the stone setts of the street below. The church has been here since 1861. Opposite is the old Mawdsley Street Congregational Church. The County Grammar School is beyond St Patrick's, across the road from the former Inland Revenue building. In the distance, on Bradshawgate, is one of Bolton's best loved cinemas. The Lido belonged to an era when we had lovely names for our picture palaces. Was it not more

romantic to meet your boyfriend outside the Palladium, Roxy, Majestic or Rialto than a boring Multiplex? After all, the cinema was where we did much of our courting. Usherettes played the lights from their torches onto the back row, just in case couples got too amorous. At least if you courted a lad who wore glasses you knew what was on his mind when he slipped them into his jacket pocket. He could not see as far as the Pathé News cockerel, but his vision was good enough to focus on a close up of you! Sadly, the Lido became boringly called Studios 1,2 and 3. It closed its doors for the last time in recent years.

Making a living

This 1930 scene of Deansgate, at its junction with Mealhouse Lane, shows the true nature of the British public. Workmen are hard at it. They are shovelling stones and tar into the road repairs. The steam from the tarring machine rises into the sky, mingling with that rising from the bodies of men sweating away at a tiring, backbreaking task. All the while a bobby on point duty stands to attention, totally focused on his job. He is a public servant with a duty to perform. He totally ignores the activity behind him and concentrates on keeping the traffic moving. The rest of the scene is taken up with the good old British public. They are fascinated with what is going on in front of them. They lounge over the railings and watch the men at work. Quite what is so interesting about a road repair is difficult to explain. But, it always happens. Perhaps it is something to do with taking pleasure in seeing others slave away while we stand idly by. Behind the onlookers was a clutch of different businesses. RG Connor was a diamond merchant and jeweller of some renown. Some in the crowd would have bought their hats at Dunn's, while others enjoyed a tipple from a hip flask topped up at Munro's off licence.

The powers that be seem to think the general public is both blind and gormless. The warning sign hardly gives any more information than is obvious to a two year old. Yet, we have to have a notice. It was probably more than someone's job was worth not to caution everyone that Chorley New Road was being dug up. In March 1947 the trams had just about had their day. It was time to do away with the tracks that had served the town so well, but change was in the air as we started to rebuild after the war. But for the hostilities trams would probably have been phased out sooner. Bolton's main arterial roads had seen developments over the years. The town was an important stopping place for cross country coaches in the 18th and 19th centuries. The mail coach was a common sight as it left the Swan Hotel. Passengers got off their coaches at the Man and Scythe, weary after the three day journey from London. In early Victorian times horses pulled seaside specials along the road towards Chorley and off to Southport. The men working hard on the rails and road setts would have given their eye teeth for a day by the sea. However, in March they probably would have settled for a cup of hot Oxo being advertised on the hoarding above their heads.

Below: Politicians have their soapboxes. Even those give more elevation than the simple block upon which this bobby stood. He looks more like a Subbuteo figure than someone in control of the traffic flow along Deansgate in 1927. The woman passing behind him, infant clutched to her bosom, cut an elegant figure. Her fashionable hat did not afford her very good vision, with its brim half covering her eyes. But, what did that matter? It looked smart, fashion was never meant to be practical, the look was all important. Anyway, she had the policeman to rely on for her safety. He was in charge; with one imperious sweep of a white cuff he could bring traffic to a standstill. Today, we imagine that our roads, threequarters of a century ago, were peacefully quiet thoroughfares. Whilst they may not have been packed with cars as they are now, they were still dangerous enough. Horse drawn vehicles vied with lorries and cars. Motor buses and trams competed for space. The tram cables above the policeman's head were part of an electrified system begun in 1899. By the time he went on point duty there were 60 miles of tramway in and around Bolton, carrying 58 million passengers a year. The bobby on his rostrum needed eyes in the back of his head keeping everything moving safely.

Bottom: Fold Street is now the shortest street in the town. Before it was closed off in 1969 it had been an active part of the Bolton scene. Various trades and professions flourished side by side. There were architects and solicitors' offices, alongside these the professionals could get a haircut or a meal at the hairdresser and restaurants that also plied their trade on Fold

Street. It was once called Lever Street, but was renamed in July 1806 in honour of a former vicar of Bolton parish church. Parson Folds (1755-1820) was something of a local character. Not for him a peaceful life of prayer and privation, he enjoyed a good tipple. His favourite poison was Jamaican rum, which he had specially shipped from the West Indies. Folds would collect his cask from Liverpool and then drive his cart back home, sitting astride his prized delivery. It was a real case of roll out the barrel when he got home. In 1954 workmen were taking up the old setts in the roadway. Unusually, they were made out of wood. They had been laid originally to lessen the noise for patients in the nearby Bolton Infirmary. Carts and carriages rumbling over granite setts would have unsettled the sick. It was a charitable thought, but no longer needed. The little hospital, in Nelson Square, had long ceased to function.

Above: At a first glance you would think that this picture was part of the collection of war damage photographs. The result is much the same as if a Heinkel had deposited its deadly load upon Bolton. There is rubble and debris everywhere. The date is 13 September 1957. Other than the strained relations with the Communist world, known as the cold war, we are at peace. The destruction seen here did not come from above. The problem lay beneath our feet. There had been heavy rain for several days. As workers were off to start the morning shift a hole was spotted in the ground on Fylde Street. As the day went by worried locals felt the ground shift under them. By nightfall the hole had become a crater. It stretched for 40 yards along Fylde Street and went down to a depth of 18 feet. The old sewers, dating back to Victorian times, had collapsed, bringing down the road surface with them. By a miracle no one was killed or seriously hurt. Over 100 families were evacuated, but 19 never returned. Their homes were so badly damaged that they were condemned and demolished. The workman in the foreground was obviously a technician. He was in charge of the wheelbarrow! He seemed happy in his work, but it was a time of misery for those affected by what became known as the Fylde Street Disaster.

Right: In the wee small hours of the morning some people are going about their work before most of us see the light of day. Newsagents mark up the papers for their delivery staff to push through letter boxes. At the wholesaler's traders are loading up with fruit, vegetables and flowers, ready to take them off to market. Over in Fleetwood the night's catch is being auctioned on the quayside, packed in ice and sent off to the fishmonger's slab. On Brooklyn Street, to the north of the town centre, a milkman in his float goes about his daily work. Just like Benny Hill's Ernie, his gold tops are rattling in their crate. The rows of terraced

houses are typical of those to be found in every Lancashire town. Cheap, affordable housing for the working classes, dating from the early 20th century, were the norm for many employed in the textile business. Many were back to back buildings. Others had a small flagged yard at the rear that included an outdoor toilet. Narrow passages ran beyond these yards, in between another housing terrace. Lads practised their footballing skills, kicking a tennis ball against the wall in these alleys. The milkman left the daily pintas on steps carefully donkeystoned by housewives dressed in uniform pinnies. They had usually got the stone from the rag and bone man when he swapped it for some of their junk.

Sheet music and all that jazz

A great advantage offered by small businesses is that they often are run by people who have specialist knowledge in their particular subject area, this is not always so in the case of big national businesses. This is clearly the secret of success of the music shop presently on Fold's Road, Harker & Howarth. Jack Howarth and his business partner Tom Harker were both professional musicians, Jack playing the saxophone and clarinet and Tom played the organ and banjo, so when they started their own music business shortly after the end of the second world war, they were able to split their selling duties along the lines of their own interests, Jack sold woodwind and brass instruments as well as sheet music and Tom was in charge of the pianos, organs and accordions. Naturally they were able to call upon each others' expertise whenever it was needed.

They started out in Great Moor Street, Bolton in April 1946 where they stayed for nearly three years. In those early days they concentrated their efforts mainly on musical instrument retailing. These were days filled with hard work as they

sought to get the fledgling business off the ground, establish a reputation for helpful service and invest in building up their stock of both instruments and sheet music. It was very much a concerted family effort and Mary, Jack's wife helped out in the shop on Saturdays. But in a remarkably short time their efforts were rewarded, business increased steadily and soon they were looking for larger, more prominent premises.

It was natural that they should want to be located in The Arcade, which as every long-time resident of Bolton knows was the customary meeting place for all the town's musicians and was therefore the ideal place for the siting of a music shop. And so Harker & Howarth took its place at 7 The Arcade, Bradshawgate, Bolton.

Since that time the scope of the business has steadily grown along with the developments in the music industry. When they had the idea of opening a music shop, Jack and Tom could

Above: Founders Jack Howarth (left) and Tom Harker circa 1966. Below: 7, The Arcade, early 1950s.

years trading was duly celebrated in style by everyone concerned in 1971.

Despite the achievements of all those involved in the business it was sadly announced in 1969 that the arcade was to be demolished, however new premises were soon found on Churchgate.

scarcely have had any inkling of the development of digital and electronic musical instruments, not that it was beyond their capabilities, they widened the extent of their stock to accommodate the innovations and now, without ceasing to stock the range of instruments they have had since the beginning, they now offer guitars, keyboards as well as all the associated small goods such as manuscript paper, pencils, badges, mugs, handkerchiefs and a host of similar items.

The firm has built up that good reputation they had desired to do and now musicians of all kinds, from the beginner through to those making music for their own pleasure right up to the professionals, rely on Harker & Howarth to supply what they require. People return to them again and again for their vast product knowledge, range of stock and their reputable after sales service. They undertake instrument repairs and the majority of these take place on the premises. Harker & Howarth are the largest music shop in the area, a kind of musical instrument superstore, a fact which helps them retain their advantage over their competitors.

The firm has of course benefited greatly from the knowledge, expertise and loyalty of their staff over the years and the 25

Later due to current out of town shopping trends and the provision of parking facilities, the Folds Road piano showroom underwent a total refit to accommodate all departments under one roof, and so providing a one stop music store. The opening in September 1990 was attended by the Lord Mayor of the town.

Now the second generation of Harker and Howarth are involved in the firm; Charles Harker, John Howarth and his wife Adele are building on the hard work of Tom and Jack, responding to new challenges in the spirit of their parents. They will seek to maintain all that is good and valued in the service they offer and adapt to changing circumstances and developments as they arise.

Above Left: Jack Howarth outside their Churchgate shop, 1971. Above Right: Opening day of the new shop, September 1990. Below: An interior view of the new shop in Fold's Road, 1990.

Generations of demolition

Throughout the last century, and especially in the post-war years, Bolton saw huge changes. How many buildings were demolished? Who can now say. Probably too many to count, the good swept away with the bad as old Bolton gave way inexorably to the new. That same picture has been repeated all over the country and continues to this day - albeit with a little more sensitivity than was being exhibited thirty or forty years ago.

Of course when buildings are demolished one is left with a heap of rubble. But how many people stop and ask themselves what happens to that unwanted pile of broken bricks and shattered concrete? Mostly we just don't know. As far as we are concerned it is there one day and gone the next making room for whatever modern edifice is set to replace the old. But not everyone is so ignorant as us. Someone knows what happens to all that unwanted material - not least the man who drives the lorry that comes to take it away. Maybe his name was Walter, and perhaps we should have asked him where he was going.

The name of Walter Forshaw is a familiar one on the roads in the Bolton area.

The haulage firm of Walter Forshaw Ltd, now based at 7, King Street, Westhoughton, was founded as long ago as 1898 by Walter Forshaw's father, Jesse. Originally a coal merchant, Jesse had previously worked at local coal mines before branching out on his own to become a coalman, using a horse and cart to carry his wares from place to place. There was certainly nothing wrong with being a small part of the coal industry in the closing years of

Above: Forshaw's fist coal delivery vehicle.
Below: Jesse Forshaw's father, grandfather of Walter outside the family shop and home on the corner of King Street.

Queen Victoria's reign. Lancashire ran on coal. Homes, hospitals and schools were heated by it and factories were powered by it. Who then could have predicted the disappearance of both pits and the steam engine?

Until the end of the second world war in 1945 business remained steady, but Jesse Forshaw seems to have been content with his small corner of the commercial world and made few attempts to move with the rapidly changing times. In 1943 however Jesse died.

Walter Forshaw whose name the firm bears, and his wife Annie, took over Jesse Forshaw's small business following his death and began to develop the firm. With a new generation came new ideas and with them the imagination and drive to implement them. From simply being a coal merchants Walter and Annie moved into general haulage when demand for coal began to fall and local pits began to close. Supplying and delivering building materials in the 1960s would eventually lead to work in demolition, the field which the company now specialises in.

The business had always been based on King Street, the original office being at number 16 where the Forshaws lived, until an office was opened in 1959 at 7 King Street. In 1971 a haulage depot began to be used in Bolton Road, Westhoughton when the firm moved from coal haulage into general tipping and haulage work.

Today, from having once operated just a single horse and cart, the firm uses a variety of heavy plant and eight wheeled lorries to carry construction material. Having long moved on from coal today the firm specialises in both

demolition and in the supply of reclaimed aggregates to local councils and construction companies, as well as housing associations, civil engineers, and builders.

Four generations of the family have now been involved with the business: Jesse, his son Walter, Walter's wife Annie who is still connected with the firm. And Walter and Annie's children, Harry, Keith, Dora and Joyce, all still work for the firm as do their children Karen, Andrew, Christian and Adrian.

Today this family oriented business remains one with a personal touch: and it is one of largest demolition companies in the North West to still use direct labour. But though this may be a traditional firm there is nothing old fashioned about the way the business is run: the Forshaw family aims to provide a completely efficient and up to date demolition service using the most modern equipment and techniques available.

Above left: A Forshaw vehicle dressed up for Gala Day.
Below: One of Forshaw's eight wheeled haulage vehicles.
Bottom: A High Reach machine on demolition contract.

The tools for success

A Bolton Engineering Company with long-standing connections with the aerospace and nuclear industries among others is celebrating over 35 years trading from its premises in a former textile mill in Kershaw Street.

Bob Maxwell, a Chartered Mechanical & Production Engineer, and Ken Owens, a technical representative for an engineering firm and a former toolmaker, both felt they would like to form their own company. They had come into contact with each other through direct dealings between their respective companies and went into partnership, commencing trading in 1966.

Rather than starting from scratch they bought out an existing small one-man engineering business, Aldred & Co as a going concern. In setting up they were greatly helped by Bob's cousin J D Maxwell a Chartered Accountant, who having overseen the purchase of the original firm helped them with Company Registration and advised them on financial matters. His company has served as their accountants ever since.

Purchasing an existing firm was a good starting point for the new would-be entrepreneurs as they not only acquired machinery and equipment but also the goodwill and a customer base. Unfortunately the building was too small and unsuitable so a search for alternative premises began. Eventually an ideal building was found which had served as a development department for a local weaving mill, having three floors and an area of 2,400 sq ft, being well built and equipped with electricity, water, heating and toilet facilities it appeared to be the perfect place to set up business.

These premises in Kershaw Street have served the company well since its inception. They paid £6.00 per week rent on a seven year lease at the outset for the building but were able to purchase it in 1971 for £5000. In the early days only the ground floor was used but soon additional space was required and all three floors were used. The ground floor is given over to heavier machinery, the second floor to light machinery, fitting and inspection and the top floor houses the administration side of things.

The infant company also required a name. Using letters from their own name KEn Owens and Bob MAXwell provided a suitably memorable label by which their operation could be known.

Ken invited three skilled toolmakers he knew from British Aerospace to join the new venture and in March 1966 production began. The partners decided to concentrate on toolmaking to local firms providing jigs, fixtures, tem-

Top left: *Kemax co-founder Bob Maxwell.*
Above left: *A locomotive steam manifold.*
Left: *Carbon fibre sheet manufacturing rolls.* ***Below:*** *A conductivity test rig.*

plates, press tools gauges and sub-contact manufacture. This enabled them to give a rapid response, delivery and a personal service to their customers, a policy which has been maintained over the years. The practice of re-investing profit in additional or updated machinery commenced even at this early stage and this has continued throughout the lifetime of the firm.

Ken Owens was Managing Director and took responsibility for quoting and procuring work. Bob was Works Director in charge of planning and manufacturing. The workforce gradually increased and by 1974 they were employing 20 men. They have always prided themselves on the quality of their products and their ability to specialise in 'one-offs' and small batch production. There has always been an emphasis on training apprentices to the high standard required and the on-going training of staff. The firm was a founder members of Bolton Engineering Training Group (now Alliance Learning Ltd).

Ken Owens semi retired in 1986 and unfortunately died in 1989 and Bob subsequently became the sole proprietor. He was joined by his son Stuart in 1994. They offer a personal and professional service, seeking to make their considerable expertise available to produce quality products noted for their accuracy. The skilled workforce has over 360 years of experience between them. This experience and the fact that there are two Chartered Engineers at the helm enables them to offer an advice service to customers.

The company has weathered many changes over the years, especially during the 1990s when there was an economic recession and the customer base was drastically reduced due to the decline of the engineering industry in general and the intro-

duction of numerically controlled machines. However Kemax has continued production throughout this time and whilst the workforce has naturally changed over the years due to retirements, ill health, etc, many of the employees have worked faithfully for the firm for over 30 years.

The company has taken advantage of new machinery and production methods and uses equipment which is much more sophisticated than was available in the 1960s. The high standards and experience they offer has qualified them to continually supply products to nuclear and other industries and at the present they are pursuing ISO 9002 accreditation for the excellence of their work. In addition they undertake work for the automotive, mining, power, railway, metal forming and food industries. They also offer breakdown services for local industries, and occasionally supply companies in France and the USA.

It is Kemax's achievement to be still an engineering presence in Bolton at a time when many other companies have had to close. In the future the firm wishes to continue to manufacture tools to the quality and precision that have made them a recognised name in the locality for the high standard of their engineering work. They are aiming to increase their customer base and continue the programme of re-investing profit into new machinery which has been a source of so much of their success in the past. The name Kemax will continue to be a byword for quality in the world of toolmaking.

Top left: Bob Maxwell with son Stuart.
*Above left: Perspex model centrifuge for radioactive material. **Above:** A gear inspection fixture.*
Below: Kemax Kershaw Street premises.

A fishy but fruity family tale

There will always be a living to be made from selling food. But not many will be as successful or as highly regarded as the business set up by Harry and Enid Grundy in 1971. The firm will need no introduction to the huge number of customers who make a bee-line to the Grundy stalls in Ashburn Street market, where they are a well-established presence, having been there for over 30 years.

Harry himself has been working on the market, selling fish and poultry for nearly fifty years. This makes him something of an institution. He began his working life working for S F S who had the stall adjacent to the Grundy's present site. There's not much about the market that he doesn't know by now, and he enjoys the chance to provide the residents of Bolton with good food, along with a cheery smile and a little friendly banter.

Harry and Enid started out selling fish and poultry to the people of Bolton with the intention of giving them the highest quality products at a competitive price. Such ambitions are not achieved by accident and Harry used to start his day at 5 am when he drove his van to Manchester each day to purchase supplies which had been quickly transported from the fishing ports of Aberdeen, Grimsby and Fleetwood. He would be back in time to arrange an attractive display on his market stall before the first customers arrived.

It is clear that his ambition was realised as customers liked the food he had to offer and bought it enthusiastically, impressed by the quality and freshness of the fish he had for sale. Over the years, as word got round, the number of his customers grew and the Grundys became a familiar sight in the market and their stall could be identified by the throng of people gathered round.

Seeking to build on their success, Harry and Enid decided to branch out into another line of business and endeavoured to bring the same philosophy of quality and value to selling fruit and veg as they were doing with fish and poultry. They acquired the stall in the adjoining

Above Left: Co-founder Harry Grundy. **Left:** *Stall dressed up for the Royal Wedding of HRH Prince Charles and Lady Diana Spencer in 1981.*

dressed up the stalls in an appropriately festive way. Both fish and fruit and veg stalls are frequented by shoppers from all over the North-West who prefer Grundy wares to that offered by the supermarkets. They have been fortunate in their staff over the years who have given friendly and cheerful service to the purchaser as well as a high level of knowledge about the food they were selling.

All Grundy produce, whether on the fish or fruit and veg stall, is bought in fresh almost daily. This entails attending Manchester market four times a week at 4 am to ensure they get the pick of the available supplies. This is what their customers have come to expect, after all.

market and again scored a great hit with the Bolton shoppers. In time Chris, their son, tried his hand at it during a year out before going up to university. He liked the work and for going on for twenty years now he has taken responsibility for this side of the business.

Both stalls offer the same standards of freshness and quality coupled with a wide variety of produce and well presented displays. Aromatic herbs hang down over heaps of firm cabbages, piles of plump aubergines and appetising carrots while snow-white cauliflowers form a solid looking pyramid. On the fish counter the eye is drawn from the bright shades of the smoked fish to the silver scales of the whole trout and salmon over the brightly coloured salmon steaks to the white fish. It is all truly a feast for the senses of sight and smell. The ability to provide eye-catching displays which attract the buyer is quite a gift in itself and the Grundy's are ever alert to different ways of doing just that. On the occasion of the wedding of Prince Charles and Lady Diana Spencer, they

Above: Harry and staff on the fish stall.
Left: Alison Chapman, Enid Grundy, Harry Grundy and Chris Grundy in front of the family Fruit and Veg stall.
Below: The Grundy Fruit and Veg stall run by Harry and Enid's son Chris.

Painting the town...any colour you like

Bernard Stott Decorators have been brightening up the lives of Bolton residents since 1920. The firm was founded by Bernard Stott's father and at one time father and both his sons, Bernard and Herbert were involved. During the Second World War, Bernard was drafted into the Fire Service and served in Bolton and London in this capacity. After the end of the war, Bernard and Herbert resumed their trade as painters and decorators, operating from Bernard's home in 29 Belmont Road, Bolton.

The present owner, Neville Mills started work for the company in 1950, six months after leaving school. After three months probation he was indentured and bound to the firm for 6 years, during which time he was taught the trade as a private decorator, as that was the main area in which they worked.

At that time the company consisted of Bernard, Herbert, Jack Hazledean, a Journeyman and Neville, the Apprentice.

Sadly, Herbert died approximately 1952 and after only three years with the firm, Jack was required to do his National Service, so there was only Bernard and Neville, an eighteen year old at this time, left to build up the firm's reputation. As well as helping Bernard undertake private commissions during the day, Neville attended night school two evenings a week to learn various areas of the trade, as well as the theory behind the practical work and he also added graining, paperhanging and multi-colour spray techniques to the list of his skills.

Above: Neville Mills' deed of Apprenticeship.
Below: Restoring Turton Towers to its former glory.

viding total client satisfaction. The expertise and skill acquired over a long period as well as their detailed knowledge of the trade gives them an ability to provide solutions to customers problems not offered by more recently established firms.

This expertise was demonstrated and put into practice when they were entrusted with the renovation of Turton Towers in 1985-86, a well-known local landmark. Every piece of timber in the building had to be stripped of its many coats of paint before it could be carefully restored and made to look as it probably had done when new. It has not been repainted since.

A steady slow expansion of the business in the future is what is being aimed for by the firm. Those involved in the firm have the great satisfaction of having provided a valued service to the people and institutions of Bolton and gained a stable and good living for their employees and themselves over many years. They are proud that this achievement has been built on integrity and professionalism.

The company began to prosper. Gradually Bernard expanded the scope of the work they undertook to include public and commercial ventures for schools, hospitals and other Local Authority work. The company was incorporated in 1962 and Neville was made a Director in 1967.

The business grew steadily and the next few years brought important changes with them. They moved operations to their present building in Viola Street in 1972 (it was only 100 yards up the road from where they had been before). Due to the steady increase in business, this itself was to prove inadequate over the next few years and in 1988 the building was extended, doubling its size to accommodate all the decorating equipment on one side and providing offices and the popular Trade Shop on the other.

After a satisfying lifetime of work in the decorating business, Bernard retired in 1975, leaving Neville in charge of the firm they had built up together. In 1978, he made a rather different contribution to the trade when he branched out into specialist paint supplier - JEM Paints was launched to provide a range of paints produced particularly suitable for use on wood.

Bernard Stott (Decorators) is now a medium sized firm with the aim of pro-

Above: A staff picture taken at a Christmas party.
Below: Present owners, Neville Mills, with daughter Julie and wife Edith.

An electrifying record

A name which has been a familiar one to natives of Bolton for very many decades is that of the Engineering Services Company.

The company was founded in 1922 at which time however it occupied premises in Corporation Street.

Despite the economic recession it was still a good time to enter such a business as electricity continued its gradual process of ousting gas as the power source of choice.

The firm's founders were HM Harrison, who had previously been the electrical engineer at Bessemer Furnaces then situated on the site which is now occupied by Moor Lane Bus Station, and James Makin who had been a mining surveyor with A Knowles mining engineers of Clifton.

In 1928, six years after its founding, the business moved to retail premises at 43 Market Street, and later, in 1936, on to 18/20 Market Street. The shop on Market Street sold all kinds of electrical goods and eventually became an agent for Hoover appliances as well as selling some of the earliest television sets seen in Bolton.

The business did not however simply involve the retail sales of electrical goods. The firm's true forte was electrical engineering. Some of the early contracts undertaken by the company were for the Town Hall and Civic centre during 1936-38; the Manchester Road Technical College and, post war, the reconstruction of the Ferranti's Domestic appliance factory were also important projects.

The company also provided and maintained the power and lighting for many of the area's cotton mills, and Tillotsons' offices. So successful was the business that at one time the electrical engineering side of the company had almost 100 employees.

*Top left: Co-founder James Makin pictured circa 1914-1918. **Top right**: Co-founder Mr HM Harrison, pictured with his wife. **Below left**: Enjoying a cup of tea, Mr James Makin (cup in hand) and Mr HM Harrison (back row far right). **Below**: An Engineering Service's brochure, 1925.*

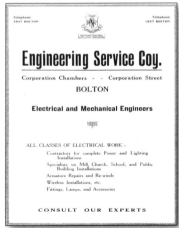

Telephone 1647 BOLTON   Telephone 1647 BOLTON

Engineering Service Coy.

Corporation Chambers - - Corporation Street
BOLTON

Electrical and Mechanical Engineers

ALL CLASSES OF ELECTRICAL WORK :-
Contractors for complete Power and Lighting Installations
Specialists on Mill, Church, School, and Public Building Installations
Armature Repairs and Re-winds
Wireless Installations, etc.
Fittings, Lamps, and Accessories

CONSULT OUR EXPERTS

As a typical family firm it was intended for HM Harrison's son to join the company after the second world war, but tragically he was killed serving in the RAF during the conflict. HM Harrison's brother WH Harrison was then invited to join the firm and he became the third partner.

In 1946 R Makin, the son of James, joined the business and eventually became Contracts Manager and later a partner, together with H Simons who had been a staff member before the war. H Simons rejoined the company after the war where he had served in the Coldstream Guards with the rank of RSM - Regimental Sergeant Major.

At the shop in Market Street the company developed its sales of records and started Bolton's own Top Ten, long before the BBC!

In those years following the end of the war the shop manager Max Lamont was a well known authority on all kinds of music from early pop to jazz, big bands and swing; he even knew the reference number of most of the records, and if he didn't stock it no-one did. All the local musicians would meet in the shop to buy and talk about the latest records, especially those recently arrived from America.

Publicity was an important part of the business. Max Lamont invited all the pop stars of the day such as Anne Shelton, Ronnie Carroll, Ronnie Hilton and many others to appear in the shop on Saturdays. Sometimes those events were all too successful and the police had to close off Market Street between the shop and the Commercial Hotel.

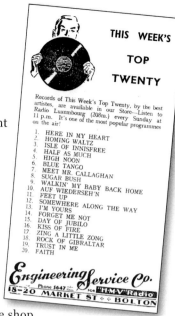

Top left: A letterhead of the former owners William Abbott & Co. ***Above:*** Engineering Service's own Top Twenty listing, from the 1950s. ***Bottom:*** A 1945 view of Market Street, the lady with a shopping bag (right) is standing outside Engineering Service's 18/20 Market Street Premises.

Bridgeman Street. Albion Works was incidentally originally called Abbots Cane Yard - where James Makin's wife had worked as a secretary before they were married. James Makin died in 1972.

Despite the popularity of the retail side of the business and burgeoning record sales the shop was sold off in 1958 to pay death duties following the death of HM Harrison.

The same year saw the electrical contracting side of the company move to its present site at Albion Works in

In 1969, prior to James Makin's death, Mr JA Flanagan had been appointed Managing Director and he acquired the controlling interest in the company in 1975. JA Flanagan's son Paul James Flanagan in his turn acquired controlling interest in the firm in 2000.

The company is still trading from the Albion Works, having evolved, over the course of its long life, from selling records and Hoover washing machines to become a thriving modern business designing and installing major commercial and industrial electrical installations including power supplies for the internet.

Top left: A 1939 view of Bolton Town Hall with Engineering Service Company sign board decorating the frontage. *Top right:* A company van pictured 1964. *Above left:* A staff picnic outing 1955. *Below:* Engineering Service's Albion Works, 2001.

Sons of the soil - digging, moving and reclaiming the earth

The Chadwick family have for four generations been making their living from the soil but the actual means by which they have done this has changed considerably over the years. Their story is one which shows them to be people who are able to see gaps in the market and respond in a way which offers the customer a service which is valued. As needs have changed, so they have been prepared to take on new challenges, but all such challenges have been met with the same attitude of seeking to offer customer satisfaction. This has been a major factor in the Chadwick success story.

Stanley Clifford Chadwick started out as a farmer in Glazebury near Warrington and became involved in general haulage, but decided to expand the haulage side of the operation and add plant hire to his services in 1944. He was joined in the venture by his son Clifford. Cliff

had left Westleigh school at 14 to drive for the Yorkshire Haulage Company, but in 1944, with his father bought a 1930 30cwt Ford and a size 10 shovel after he'd been working on McAlpine sites at Culcheth and Lytham. He was given the Ford chassis and cab in lieu of £8 wages and they towed it from Culcheth behind a BSA Sloper

motorbike. One of their first jobs was moving ash from Leigh gas works at 2/6d a time.

The business grew to such an extent that by 1959 they were looking for a much larger site and they moved to their present location in Manchester Road, Leigh in 1959, and later expanded to another waste transfer station and scrap yard in Breightmet, Bolton.

Stanley retired in 1965 by which time his grandson Michael was involved in the business. The family tradition continues today and the fourth generation of Chadwicks is currently making their own contribution to the family firm, Sean at Bolton and Gary at Leigh. Each succeeding generation can build on the success of their parents' and grandparents' efforts and customers trust the family name as they associate the name Chadwick with reliable service.

The nature of the business has gradually evolved over the years, it started out as a haulage firm then they branched out into plant hire and in 1960 they went into skip hire. Since then this side of the business has expanded to such an extent that they presently have no fewer than 750 skips.

Top right: *An early S.C.Chadwick & Sons business card.*
Above: *Two Chadwick lorries pictured in 1946.*
Bottom left: *A Chadwick tractor from the 1940s.*
Below: *Michael Chadwick at work, 1966.*

They have adopted the slogan, 'Skips big or small, we do them all!'

They can supply plant and skips to locations within a 30 mile radius of Bolton/Leigh, and pride themselves on being able to offer a quality, reliable service unmatched in the vicinity. They feel no one can offer the same level of service as consistently as they can, and the many customers who come back to them again and again obviously agree.

Sean had the idea to expand the business by going into the scrap metal trade which they did in the last decade. This has proved to be a shrewd move and this area accounts now for more than 20 per cent of the firm's turnover. In fact it is this side of things which is set to see further increases with the growing national and international concerns for all things 'green'. There is considerable and growing interest in recycling anything

which can be reused, so scrap metal and other material recycling is clearly an industry of the future, along with land reclamation undertakings, which the firm is also considering.

They use a range of skiploaders between 7.5-18 ton and 17-32 ton hooklifts for the collection and distribution of

*Left: The first skip loading system developed and made by Clifford Chadwick. **Below:** Founder Stanley Clifford Chadwick with grandson Michael and great grandson Sean. **Bottom:** The Chadwick waste transfer station and scrap yard site, Breightmet, Bolton.*

waste and scrap. A wrecker truck with Hiab for aluminium can recycling and similar jobs, a 6 wheel tipper for muck-away jobs and various items of plant that are used in waste transfer stations such as a hydraulic crane fitted with grabs and magnet equipment, two loading shovels, two forklifts. All these are employed for the collection and dispatch of raw materials and taken to their own transfer stations and scrap yards.

The volume of work is divided between industrial waste which accounts for about 65 per cent of the total, building waste, taking about 30 per cent and the remaining five per cent by the private household sector.

Residents of Bolton and Leigh may well be familiar with the sight of the bright orange and white Chadwick trucks which are to be seen on the roads in the area and these are a source of justifiable pride on the part of the Chadwick family. In 1993 Sean entered one such eye-catching lorry in a national lorry livery competition and took third prize in the 7.6-17 ton category. He was invited to collect his prize in person at the awards ceremony which was held in the Park Lane Hotel in London. Sean took his grandad, Cliff, along as his guest. They both felt very honoured by the award. The occasion prompted a write-up in the Leigh Journal soon afterwards.

The Chadwick reputation rests on their reliability and their ability to do what they say they will. With such a long history of satisfied customers and the intention of being there to meet changing needs in society and industry, Chadwicks can look forward to continuing the great family tradition for many years (and for many generations?) to come.

Above left: Chadwicks first custom built vehicle.
Above right: Clifford, Michael, Gary and Sean.
Below: A section of Chadwicks Livery, 1980s.
Bottom: The Chadwick family today, from left to right , Michael, Sean, Gary and Clifford.

Moving around, moving on

A Bolton haulage business operating from Long Lane, Westhoughton, Bolton is providing work for the fourth generation of the founder's family, transporting goods made in the Bolton area to destinations near and far. It is a story which has developed over a period spanning nearly eighty years, and one which has seen many changes and developments over the years.

It all began when William Allen (a coal merchant) procured an ex-army Pagefield with solid tyres towards the close of the first world war, and used it to transport coal to the local cotton mills. He was based at Astley Bridge at this time.

William's son Dan ran the haulage business till 1943. Tom Allen (Dan's brother) acquiring a fleet of Albion trucks, was responsible for the firm until his death in 1969 leaving his sons Richard and William at the helm.

The original premises soon became inadequate for their purposes and so only three years after the firm began it moved from Astley Bridge to Wardle Street, Darcy Lever in 1920 where it remained until 1954.

Other moves have been necessary as the firm developed. In 1954 it moved to Cannon Street, Bolton where it traded for ten years before moving back to Waters Meeting in Astley Bridge in 1965, as more space was necessary with the undertaking of storage facilities and articulated road vehicles.

The most recent move being forced by a Compulsory Purchase Order in 1997 was to Long Lane, Westhoughton where the new location is particularly beneficial to the

Above: A 1940s road transit vehicle.
Below: The ex-army vehicles purchased by William Allen.

firm as it is located adjacent to the Wingates Industrial Park, and yet still enabling them to continue to serve the Bolton area industries.

But the site of the business is not the only thing to have changed over the course of time. From the first ex-army truck, Allen's have gradually increased and modernised their vehicles up to the present day when they have an impressive fleet of Mercedes and Volvo trucks.

No-one will be surprised to learn that transporting coal is also no longer a part of their business, nowadays they chiefly handle the transport of industrial doors, structural steel, workwear, pharmaceuticals and textiles from local firms.

The firm has grown during the course of its history by offering good service at a competitive price. Plans for future development will no doubt include continuing this tradition.

Richard Allen and his son Peter, the fourth family generation, now manage the business and alongside transport and distribution, have under the same umbrella at Westhoughton an active storage facility, with plans for further expansion.

This page: The William Allen fleet of the new millennium.

Caged lightning,
the power of the past-tomorrow

Perhaps no other source of motive power has both a history and a future that compares with the story of the electric storage battery. Since its invention and development in the 18th and 19th centuries it has made an immense contribution to the world's social and industrial revolutions. Today it is the powerful heart of every kind of battery-electric vehicle and machine in the world.

Bolton's Chloride Motive Power company - CMP Batteries Ltd - is based in Salford Road, Over Hulton and is at the leading edge of such technology; but how did both the company and the electric battery industry begin?

The battery has its origins in the late 18th century. A lively debate between two leading Italian scientists of the day, Luigi Galvani and Alessandro Volta, promoted a great deal of research and ultimately led to today's huge battery industry.

Galvani found that by connecting dissimilar metal probes to the muscles of dead frogs he could make them twitch, and he speculated that electricity was the cause. Volta rejected the theory, but from Galvani's experiment he developed the world's first concept of electricity (and incidentally in the process Galvani's work also inspired Mary Shelley to write her classic Gothic novel Frankenstein).

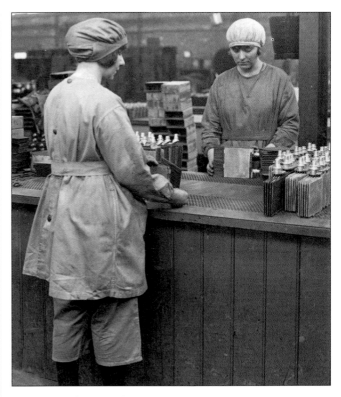

Above: Early manufacturing.
Below: A delivery by horse and cart in 1897.

Another most significant development was the concept of the tubular plate, which in its crudest form appeared as a set of parallel perforated lead tubes some time in the 1880s.

Almost immediately however the perforated lead tube was replaced by an asbestos sheath, the forerunner of the present day plate, offering a type of plate which was more robust and more efficient in terms of its capacity to weight ratio for motive power applications than either the Planté or the flat plate. By the turn of the century the ebonite tube had been introduced which would not give way to the gauntlet tube until the early 1960s.

There followed one of the most exciting periods in scientific research ever known.Volta went on to produce his famous Voltaic pile, thereby helping to discover that chemical energy can be converted to electrical power - the very first example of what we today would describe as a storage battery.

France however, not Italy, was home to the very first practical battery. A Belgian, Gaston Planté who was working in France, demonstrated the first lead acid battery in 1861. He discovered that by passing an electrical current through metal plates for a long period he was able to convert the surface of one plate to lead dioxide (the positive plate) and the surface of the other plate to spongy lead (the negative plate).

This combination produced an electrical current when the two plates were connected to an external circuit. As the only sources of charging available to Planté were the early primary batteries (i.e. those which cannot be recharged) the use of his cells was however limited to laboratory experiments until the later invention of the Gramme generator in 1873.

Planté's early battery was the basis for further work by a Frenchman, Fauré, who in the early 1880s produced an alternative flat plate design using lattice type grids instead of Planté's solid plates of lead.

Into these lattices Fauré applied lead-oxide in paste form and this design formed the forerunner of today's lead acid battery. Fauré's design had the advantage of having less weight in the plates and used a smaller space for the same energy output.

Above: CMPs original greenfield site at Over Hulton.
Below: Construction of the new site at Over Hulton 1975.
Bottom: Works Manager Norman Frost (left) and General Manager Dennis Howarth (right), with the first cell produced at the new Over Hulton site in 1978.

The last decade of the 19th century was a period of great exploitation of the many advances being made in the world of science; one important practical application of the early electric storage batteries would be the electric car.

The first battery powered car was built by a Professor Ayrton in 1888, and in England elegant electric Broughams were produced by Walter Bersey. New York saw the world's first ever horseless Hansom cab, the Morris and Salom Electric, in 1896. In 1899 a Belgian named Camille Jenatzy actually held the world land speed record for the flying kilometre in his electric racer Le Jamais Contente or 'The Never Content'.

For about 30 years from 1890 electric cars were as common on England's roads as their petrol driven rivals. In those early days of motoring many owners preferred 'electrics' for their ease of driving, relative silence, reliability and smooth running. Only with the greater engineering advances made by petrol vehicle manufacturers following the first world war and greater ease of refuelling would eventually make the internal combustion engine increasingly popular.

Today the most common electric vehicle still seen on our roads is the electric milk float. Why have they survived? The simple answer is economics. Milk delivery is a unique operation. The wear and tear on an internal combustion engine, with its many moving parts, in such an intensely stop start operation is enormous. The simpler electric vehicle is far better suited to that kind of activity.

The Chloride Electrical Storage Syndicate was formed in 1891 and manufacturing of industrial batteries began two years later at Clifton Junction near Swinton, Manchester. In subsequent years the business would move many times, though mainly continuing to be based in Lancashire.

Batteries, made using lead and acid and encased in ebonite boxes with pitch sealed lids, were always assembled on site. The basic ingredients have remained the same although today the boxes are made not from ebonite but of polypropylene with heat sealed lids.

The war years of 1939-45 accelerated technological advances in process engineering, and also saw the introduction of new materials and handling techniques which were the forerunners of today's modern logistics solutions.

From those early origins the present Chloride Motive Power company eventually emerged. In 1978 the business moved to premises built on a greenfield site at Over Hulton. In 1989 it became an independent company - CMP Batteries Ltd.

Since 1978 CMP Batteries Ltd have manufactured enough battery cells to stretch from Bolton Town Hall to Sydney Opera House. It is proud to say that the quality of its products is world renowned - many of its batteries last up to seven years and some in excess of twenty, with an

Above: *Ingredients of a lead-acid battery.*
Below left: *A low maintenance battery and battery charger.* **Below:** *Manufacturing in the 21st century.*

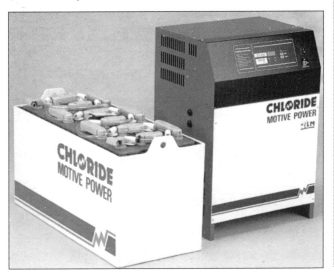

the firm from his early twenties and was wholly in charge by 1966 when the firm became a limited company.

Well before then however, in 1954, Louis Manfredi had found himself a redoubtable Italian wife, Luisa, who would be a powerhouse of energy working in the family cafe,

The firm's customers include small multiple retailers, garden centres, theme parks and the inevitable mobile ice cream vans whose diesel engines and musical tannoy systems have long since replaced the ice boxes and hand bells of the romantic, exotic figure of the Hokey-pokey man.

helping make ice-cream as well as organising mobile sales. More than forty years after her marriage Luisa would still be insisting on doing her stint in the firm.

The following years would be ones of growth. Not even the power cuts and three day weeks of the 1970s could slow that progress. In 1973 the firm moved to new premises built on land at 25, Deane Church Lane.

Though over the years the firm would switch its commercial emphasis to becoming a supplier and distributor of frozen products from a variety of producers it still continued to be a maker of ice-cream in its own right.

Today the recipes introduced by Guiseppe for his famous ice-cream have changed little, although skimmed milk powder is now used instead of milk straight from the cow.

Today the Manfredi company continues to progress by embracing new technology and ideas whilst jealously guarding and maintaining its reputation as a manufacturer of quality traditional ice cream.

Understanding customers' needs and speed of service are hallmarks of a business which intends to maintain a steady growth in the years still to come. So buy a Manfredi ice cream, then shut your eyes and lick it - and just let its inimitable taste unwrap your happy memories of childhood.

Top: A van from the 1960s.
Below left: Peter Manfredi, Managing Director, 2001.
Below: Work being carried out during the move to Deane Church Lane.

Best foot forward

The tradition of bespoke and orthopaedic shoemaking by the Whittaker family goes back to 1923 when Percy Whittaker began making shoes in a shed at the back of his home in Vallets Lane, Bolton. It expanded when Percy's son, Jack started up the retail side of the business, having joined his father when he was 14 to learn the trade. He was called up to serve in the Second World War and was taken prisoner by the Japanese.

He opened a shop on St George's Road in 1952 with just £210 worth of shoes. The years after the war were difficult ones as those who lived through them know only too well, and there was a particular problem in tracking down suppliers for the business at that time; often shoes were brought to Bolton personally carried on the bus from Manchester by members of the Whittaker family.

Eighteen years later Jack moved to the present site on Deansgate where his daughters, Judith and Diane, continue the business. Although the tradition of hand-made shoes has disappeared, they offer Ladies and Mens shoes in addition to the firmly established Childrens department. Many of those children continue to shop into adulthood as the personal touch has always been a major feature of the service.

Although Jack is now retired, customers still ask about him and speak of how much they appreciated his personal service and kindness over many years. It is, of course, a tradition his daughters are eager to continue into the third generation as they offer to the people of Bolton and the Northwest a combination of professional fitting skills and excellent customer service.

Above: *Jack Whittaker.*
Below: *Whittakers shop front, Deansgate.*

Quality and service of yester-year

Buying furniture is a tricky business. You have to live with the results for years. But at least in Bolton we know where to go for the best.

Gregory & Porritts is a name which has been familiar to generations of Bolton residents for well over a century.

The name has been synonymous with quality retailing in the town since 1895 and today its Knowlsley Street store is loaded from top to bottom with the most beautiful furniture - from traditional to modern - with most of the famous names included. Nor does it end there with the firm carrying catalogues from most manufacturers, so that what the customer sees on display in the store is only a small part of what is on offer.

Founded by two local families, the firm originally traded from Bolton Market Hall before making a move to premises in Great Moor Street in 1925.

The range of goods stocked by Gregory & Porritts was very wide and the prices low with a 'Penny bazaar' theme. With true Lancashire get up and go more and more goods were being added to the firm's range, and sales increased in proportion. Despite its modest 'market stall' start the business continued to prosper and despite the depression years followed by the second world war it managed to enjoy steady growth through the 1930s and 40s.

Astonishingly, despite such modest origins, by the 1940s around 60 stores in the North West were trading under the Gregory & Porritts name including outlets in Blackpool, Chorley, Preston and even 'over the hills' in Bradford.

What has been the secret of the firm's longevity? Perhaps the store's well known slogan 'Our name is your guarantee' says it all. The firm's reputation has spread until its name has become known far and wide; today Gregory & Porritts vans deliver as far away as Wales, Southern England and Scotland. And it is hardly surprising: when it comes to furnishing one's home with the finest quality at competitive prices and with the best service there is only one place to visit in Bolton - Gregory & Porritts.

Top Left: *A certificate presented to Gregory & Porritts in September 1909.* ***Above:*** *Store Director, John Sharples.* ***Below:*** *Gregory & Porritts Knowsley Street store.*

A long mule ride

In December 1999 the Richard Threlfall Group Ltd celebrated the eve of the new millennium by moving premises for the first time in 164 years. The new premises are in Lynstock Way, Lostock six miles West of Bolton: the original Bridgeman Place Works back in Bolton are divided into smaller units and rented out.

Originally known world-wide as a textile engineering company, with its origins in 1834, the company was first incorporated as Richard Threlfall (Holdings) Ltd in 1948.

From 1959 however the company entered a period of diversification. It played a decreasing role in the manufacture of textile machinery,

Renting out the old premises and extra space in the new factory have led to the development of the third company in the Threlfall group - RT Estates Ltd - which runs alongside GB Silicone Technology Ltd and Orseal Ltd, respectively, the liquid silicone rubber and pigmentation specialists, and the valve distribution arms of the group.

but although it had made its last Threlfall mule in 1932, the last ring spinning frame manufactured by the company did not leave Bridgeman Place until 1978.

Threlfall's had earlier begun to buy other firms, adding airport ground equipment and mining equipment to its range. In 1965, after experimenting with valve design, the company won orders from the Ministry of Defence for valves for use on British submarines and ships. The 'Orseal Valve' would eventually be supplied to 11 other navies throughout the world and would also find markets in chemical plants, fire-fighting services, the gas industry and offshore installations.

Top: *A Threlfall 'Special' Mule from the 1890s.*
Above: *Richard Threlfall's signature, 1835.*
Below: *Where it started, Richard Threlfall's house and works Bridgeman Place, Salop Street.*

The slow down in offshore development has led to a refocusing of the valve business back to distributing lower value valves - the only part of the group still remaining from pre-1980.

Work with rubber sealants would lead in turn to an ever increasing interest in liquid silicone rubber, and in 1985 to the formation of GB Silicone Technology Ltd.

The distribution of liquid silicone rubber has continued to expand, not least to the Aerospace industry. Rubber compounding and a pigment dispersion service supply coloured pigments to the rubber industry has also become a central activity. A special products division carries out extra operations on mouldings and extrusions such as cutting, punching and adhesive backing: customers include those involved in the manufacture of veterinary and healthcare products, food manufacturing equipment and hydraulics.

But who was Richard Threlfall? The young man whose name would become known to generations of Bolton residents was just 21 years old when Samuel Crompton died in 1827. Richard was employed at the Bolton Works manufacturing cotton spinning machinery and his inventive turn of mind soon led to his name appearing on a joint patent for 'self actors' - an improvement of spinning machines.

Top: Former owners, Mr William Hurst (above) and his son Richard Robert Augustus Hurst. Right: Details of a Single-Speed Mule, low headstock.
Below: A specification sheet dated 1834. Below right: A Single and Double-Speed Mule (tall headstock).

By 1834 Richard Threlfall and two partners had taken a plot of land at Bridgeman Place in Bolton-le-Moors and erected several buildings there. Bridgeman Place would eventually be known throughout the world wherever Mule spinning was carried out.

Threlfall's partners soon left leaving him in sole ownership; he would lead the firm until his death in 1868 at the age of 62. During that time the firm grew to have an immense reputation . The Threlfall Mule would become specially noted for spinning fine yarns.

The firm made drawing frames, slubbing frames, Jack frames and mules but from 1880 it concentrated on the mule which it developed to the highest standard of perfection and at one time 400s counts (or over 190 miles in lb of cotton) were being spun on Threlfall's hand mules.

After the death of Richard Threlfall, whose two sons Richard and Fred had both died in early manhood, the business was carried on by his executors and later by trustees, amongst them

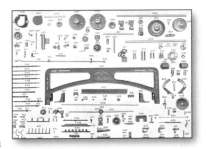

Dr James Dorrien the famous Bolton doctor and Francis McCormick the noted provisions merchant. In 1883 however Richard Threlfall's son-in-law William Hurst became the proprietor.

WilliamHurst, despite being only 24, became a worthy successor to Richard Threlfall and continued the policy of

investment and improvement, inventing several major improvements to the firm's products himself.

In 1906 after 23 years at the helm William Hurst died after a brief illness and his widow and son, Augustus, took over.

Richard Robert Augustus 'Gus' Hurst would remain at the head of the company for many decades. It was during his tenure that a serious fire destroyed many of the original buildings on the night of 31st December 1910. Sadly most of Richard Threlfall's own drawings, many historic documents, details of early patents and inventions as well as old ledgers and books were lost in the blaze leaving the recorded history of textile engineering in Bolton much the poorer.

More critically for the firm the damage was massive: the mill chimney had collapsed, walls had fallen in; the only good thing was that with the works being closed early for New Year's Eve no-one was inside. The cost of the damage was estimated at £10,000 and 250 men were thrown out of work.

Fortunately fire insurance covered the damage and Gus Hurst threw himself into reconstruction and modernisation. That modernisation included the installation of electricity, doing away with steam engines with the odd result that although the rebuilding in 1912 included a brand new chimney it would never be used except to advertise the firm's name.
Gus Hurst had been born in 1879 and had served his apprenticeship at Threlfall's. His father ensured that he worked in every department and was treated as no

differently to any other apprentice. No favours were asked or given and Gus's wage was no higher than any other apprentice. William had been a strict and sometimes stern parent and there was a lot of William in Gus which often led to angry exchanges flying between them.

When William Hurst died however Gus was eminently suited to taking over the reins.

After dealing with the disaster of the great fire the manufacture of textile equipment soon had to take second place to making munitions on the outbreak of war in 1914. Threlfall's machinery was turned to making bombs, fuses and shells. After the war, in 1918, business briefly boomed. Mules all over the world had not been repaired or maintained for four years; 1918 also saw the birth of Richard Threlfall Hurst who would one day, still far in the future, take on his father's mantel.

Like all businesses Threlfall's struggled to survive through the 1920s and the depression of the 1930s. When the second world war broke out in 1939 Threlfall's once again abandoned textile equipment for munitions. The company made shell cases for 25 lb field guns and for the multipurpose 17 lb gun. Rockets were made for use on navy vessels as well as the army's Wallbuster rocket. Axle trees for field artillery were also made as well as various aircraft components. As a

Above: A view of the expanded Bridgeman Place Works.
Below: The Threlfall Ring Spinning Frame.

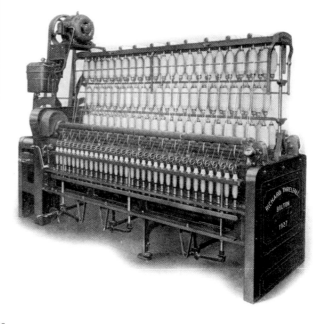

After the retirement of Hamo and Dickie in the 1980s the business would be run by Dickie's son Richard and his son-in-law David Speak, who until his own retirement in 2000 was responsible for the valve business. Richard Hurst, also a graduate engineer having joined, the firm in 1980, eventually taking over as Chairman on the death of his father in 1996.

How have GB Silicone Technolgy Ltd and Orseal Ltd survived and thrived when so many firms have fallen by the wayside? The answer was supplied by Dickie Hurst in the mid 1980s 'Lines introduced in the last five years account for 70 per cent of our production... we have changed and hopefully will continue to change'.

Threlfall's has certainly changed dramatically from its origins; and by continuing the tradition of innovation established by its founder, the Threlfall group has ensured itself a fine future as well as an impressive past.

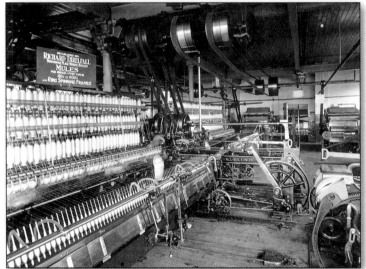

result of the shortage of men 250 women were taken onto manufacture these sinews of war.

Augustus Hurst died in 1959 and the helm was taken over by his son, Richard 'Dickie' Threlfall Hurst. Dickie Hurst and his sisters had been directors of the firm since its incorporation in 1948 and he had worked for the company since gaining his degree in science at the University of Manchester. Augustus Hurst's death came at the time when the cotton industry had begun its decline. Dickie Hurst supported by his sisters and aided by Managing Director Hamo Percival who would lead the drive for diversification which would lead to today's company.

*Top left: An early Ring Frame. **Top right:** Richard 'Dickie' Hurst OBE, Chairman 1959-1996. **Above left:** A mule. **Below:** A Swedish Navy Submarine, for which Threlfall's manufacture valves.*

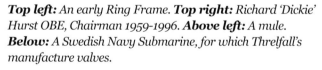

In the market

Markets, what memories they hold. Who can ever forget their early visits to them accompanying mother on her weekly shopping trips? Remember the aroma of fresh oranges, the scent of sticky sweets lingering in the air and the sound of stallholders shouting their wares?

There are now two markets in the centre of Bolton: the Market Hall along with Bolton Market in Ashburner Street. The oldest of these is Bolton Market which has been located at various points a round the town centre since the town was first granted a market charter in 1251. The retail market would be based in the Churchgate area from 1251 to 1826 and the fish market there from 1826 to 1865. In the very earliest times the market was held in front of the parish Church but as Bolton grew in size and population the market extended along Churchgate, Deansgate and later 'Windy Bank' (Bank Street) and Bradshawgate. These four principal streets met at a market cross which stood for three hundred years until it was replaced in 1786 by a larger one with circular stone steps. On the cobblestones of the market place also stood the old wooden stocks with accommodation for two villains and which served the dual purpose of both punishing malefactors and entertaining market goers.

The site of the original marketplace can still be seen. The ancient stocks may have disappeared along with the old cross but the original street pattern remains - though Bradshawgate has been substantially widened and it, together with Churchgate and Deansgate, no longer form the centre of the town. The commemorative bronze obelisk topped by a bronze cross given by a local benefactor which marks the site where old market was, now details the main events in the history of Bolton from 1253 to 1901.

At the site of the Market Cross in 1651, James, Earl of Derby was executed for his part in the bloody massacre of Bolton folk during the English Civil War.

In 1826 the market moved to New Market Place which is the site on which Bolton Town Hall now stands in Victoria Square.

Left: Bolton New Market Hall, opened 19th December, 1855. **Right:** *Great Moor Street market in 1890.* **Below:** *The Market Hall, Knowsley Street, 1895.*

began to crowd the surrounding streets becoming a source of inconvenience to both business and traffic. The New Market Place site then became a wholesale-only market until 1871 in which year it moved to the Great Moor Street enclosure where it would stay until 1932.

The Great Moor Street site was bought by the corporation for £9,000. It had been occupied by Coronation Mills together with some cottages. The buildings were soon demolished and an open market built enclosed by brick walls with stone copings and iron railings. Although originally only wholesale traders used Great Moor Street, later it was to open on Saturdays and some weekdays for retail trade. Great Moor Street would be the last of the true open markets in Bolton's history.

*Top: Market trading in Great Moor Street,1920. **Above left:** A view inside Market Hall before the alterations. **Below:** After alterations, 1938.*

New Market Place was claimed to be the finest open air market in the country. At the opening Benjamin Hick of the Soho Iron Works presented a gas lamp which was to be a feature of the square for many years; later his son John paid for a circular water trough round the base of the lamp. Sometime after the opening a 'People's Drinking Fountain' was erected near the lamp, taking the form of a bronze nymph pouring water from a vase, made at the Coalbrook Works, the cost was raised by subscriptions from the town's workers.

The 'new' market was a retail and wholesale market from 1826 until 1855 when the Market Hall first opened in 1855 in Knowsley Street to serve as a covered retail market. The reason for the move seems to have been the New Market becoming a victim of its own success as stalls and carts

In 1865 a fish market was built in Bridge Street next to the still-new Market Hall and this too stood until 1932 when the current 'traditional' market site at Ashburner Street was opened. The old, 1865, fish market was demolished to permit street widening; it was not missed: there had been many complaints that is was both malodorous and unhygienic; upon its demolition business was transferred to Ashburner Street.

In 1894 the blank walls of the Market Hall in Knowsley Street were pierced to provide the shops which are there today. The Market Hall also underwent a major refurbishment in August 1935 and the Hall was officially reopened on 5th April 1938 by the mayor. More recently the Market Place Shopping Complex was built onto the Market Hall and opened by HM the Queen in 1988.

The Market Hall had been built on a large plot of uneven land lying between Deansgate and the River Croal upon which previously existed a large number of decrepit buildings, including cramped and unsanitary cottages arranged in damp, dark courts - one being known as 'Dog Row'.

At the time the Market Hall was built not only were the poor dwellings demolished and replaced by superior ones but roads were also constructed to allow easier communication between Great and Little Bolton: in the process 1,700 cellar dwellings were closed and a sanitary scheme introduced. All the various works cost £100,000. Of that sum £14,000 was spent on the construction of Knowsley Street. The huge work was finished at the close of 1855 and the new Market Hall opened for business with an impressive ceremony in December of that year.

For many years the Market Hall would not only be one of the most attractive halls of its kind in the country but at 294 feet long, 219 feet wide and 51 feet high it was also the largest, covering some 1.5 acres.

As the provision in Great Moor Street was proving inadequate, the Bolton Corporation Acts of 1922 and 1925 made provision for a new wholesale and retail market to replace the old one. Part of what was known as the Bessemer Site on Blackhorse Street was chosen for the new market by the Markets Committee. The old Bolton forge had closed and the land it had occupied between Railway Street, Moor Lane and Blackhorse Street was an ideal site for a new market. The scheme was also part of a much larger scheme for rebuilding the centre of Bolton.

The new market building cost £101,950, clearing and preparation of the site £13,363 and paving and sewer

Above: Around the stalls of Knowsley Street in 1960.
Below left: Ashburner Street fish market, March 1964. Below right: A view from Knowsley Street, September 1962.

provision £10,727 - a grand total of £126,040. That sum however did not include the cost of the land which was compulsorily acquired by the Corporation.

The new buildings included a wholesale fruit and vegetable market, wholesale and retail fish market and a miscellaneous retail market. Except for a small open section all branches of the market were now brought under cover and protected from the weather, though the garden plant traders continued to trade outside on a cobbled path across the road next to the bus station it effectively swept away the last vestige of open air trading that had been the traditional market setting since the thirteenth century.

The site of the old wholesale market behind Newport Street was sold by the markets committee for use as a car park.

The new building would cover an area more than twice that of the old wholesale fruit and vegetable and fish markets. The wholesale fruit and vegetable market at the east end of the building had an inside ground floor hall surrounded on three sides by a continuous three storey building divided into 16 units, the ground floor having steel roller shutters.

Across Ashburner Street from the market were once the Markets Superintendent's office and the weights and measures Department building later relocated in the Town Hall Crescent as well as a public weigh office and weigh bridge. Behind and alongside those buildings was a large paved square used normally as a car park and for the annual Summer and New Year Fairs.

Bolton Market in Ashburner Street is now a retail fruit and vegetable market and is no longer a wholesale market.

Will Bolton's markets survive long enough to celebrate a thousand years of history? Of course. Supermarkets, hypermarkets and out of town shopping malls are so far nothing more than a short lived fashionable trend. Institutions which can count their years not in decades but centuries are unlikely to disappear in the face of such juvenile competition. Our grandchildren can surely look forward to visiting Bolton's markets with as much enjoyment as did our grandparents.

Above: Entertaining the shoppers at Ahsburner Street outside market, August 1998. Below: An interior view of Market Hall, 1990s.

Timberrr...

There's something about the smell of freshly sawn timber. A joiner cutting into wood with a saw releases a fragrant scent of resin that simply cannot be replicated. That aroma seems to stimulate the desire, particularly amongst men of a certain age, to want to get out their own saws, hammers and nails. That DIY instinct has become ever more urgent in recent decades. Why should that be so? Who can say. Maybe it is the cost of labour which has made employing tradesmen to work for us prohibitive, perhaps it is the plethora of television programmes exhorting us to do up our homes - the latest in a long line of DIY programmes which began with Barry Bucknall more years ago than most of us care to remember. Or perhaps it is the fact that so many of us no longer do manual jobs in our working lives and feel the need to use our hands to make us feel like 'real' people again.

On the face of it 1960 was a good year to start a new business. Not long before Harold Macmillan had told us we had never had it so good. And whilst those may not have been his exact words the underlying principle was true. After decades of recession and poverty followed by the shortages of second world war and post-war austerity suddenly things were looking good. Unemployment was at a record low and real incomes had begun to rise to levels previously unknown to working men. And if the working man was coming to terms with a new financial prosperity just maybe he, or perhaps his wife, would be thinking about making those long delayed home improvements. But would a Lancashire man beat a path to Anthony Axford's door or prefer to spend his money on the new consumer goods which were now becoming widely available: washing machines, refrigerators and televisions ?

In the first week of opening Anthony's shop took just £13.

Whatever the reasons for its popularly of DIY has boomed and with it companies which supply us with the materials necessary to pursue our obsession. The year 2000 saw a celebration for one of those firms, Bolton's Anthony Axford Ltd timber company, as the business marked its fortieth successful year of operation.

It was in 1960 when the firm's founder, Anthony Axford, bought a small shop in Farnworth. For the previous four years he had been a self-employed joiner in the area. Anthony decided to buy his own premises and open a DIY shop in a block of terraced shops in Albert Road, Farnworth.

For a short while it looked as though his business gamble might have been a mistake: perhaps record players would take precedence over fitting new shelves. Fortunately however people seem to have decided they could do both. And even those who had decided that buying a telly was their number one priority soon found that Barry Bucknall and his ilk were inspiring them in ways they might never previously have considered.

Above: Staff in the early days from left to right; Anthony Axford, James Heaher, Edward Slater circa 1966.

From such small beginnings a mighty business would grow. Lancashire men and Lancashire builders did beat a path to Anthony's door. In the years following the establishment of that first shop Anthony Axford gradually took over the other seven shops in the block containing his original premises. Business continued to boom and in 1978 Anthony was able to buy even more space for his expanding company, this time in Louisa Street in Walkden. Just two years later the whole operation became a limited company. By the time of incorporation the business which had once had a turnover of just £13 a week was turning over £700,000 a year.

Under Anthony Axford's guidance, and assisted by a small staff of just nine, the business continued to prosper and to grow at a remarkable rate. Eventually it became apparent that even larger premises needed to be found if expansion was to continue. Fortunately a nearby engineering firm, based on a site of some two acres, went into receivership and Anthony Axford Ltd snapped up the vacant lot in King Street. But still the staggering success continued, and with it the need to expand still further.

In 1991 the company acquired a small merchant outlet in the aptly named Bark Street, Bolton then known as

Tudor Timbers (which now trades under the Axford name). Four years later, anticipating even more growth, the Bark Street branch was moved to larger premises across the road, to what was formerly the GPO garage - the firm and Bolton residents are now reaping the benefits.

The company's main business remains the supply of timber, plywood, doors and builders' hardware. That simple description

Left: The Atlas Works pictured in 1983. Below: 149 to 161 Albert Road pictured prior to demolition in 1983.

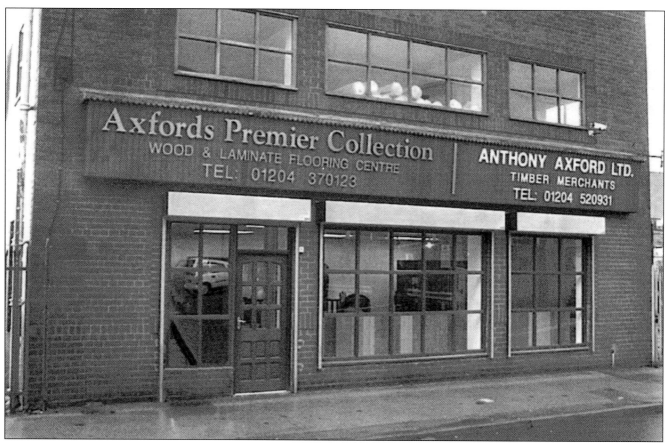

however hardly does justice to the range of products available. Timber can be home-grown or imported and the team at each branch will cut the wood to any length or size required.

Cutting wood to length however is the least of the firm's skills: staff will machine architectural mouldings, door casings, window sections, tongue and groove boards or cut any section of timber a customer requires.

In addition to timber the firm also supplies a dizzying array of related products such as doors, laminated flooring, a large selection of DIY goods, kitchens and plumbing goods - even cookers and washing machines.

The company deals with all manner of customers including large and small building firms, industry and local councils. As well as its 'trade' customers the business also has thriving retail sales selling products and services to the public at large. With such a wide range of products and so broad a customer base it is

little wonder that the firm has expanded and continues to expand with an impressive record for diversification.

In the final five years of the 20th century the company would invest £700,000, ploughing money back into the business to buy new buildings, property and equipment. The next project would be the building a new sales centre at the Walkden branch.

Since its birth the extraordinary growth rate of the company was such that in the 1980s and 1990s the number of people employed increased more than six-fold. Between the three premises (the Head office in Farnworth and the branches in Walkden and Bolton) the business now has 60 staff ranging from joiners and machinists and their respective apprentices, 'visual stress graders', forklift truck and lorry drivers and their motor mechanics as well as trained sales and office staff. A far

> *In the years following establishment of that first shop, the firm gradually took over the other six shops in the block*

Top: The premises on Bark Street, Bolton.

118

cry indeed from that single self-employed joiner who started the whole enterprise back in 1960.

With a record of such continuous growth and development it is clear to anyone who knows the business that Anthony Axford and his firm have not only found their place in the market but have demonstrated the skills, service and business acumen which are essential to every truly successful venture.

Will the company continue to grow? It seems more than likely; whilst the building industry may be enormously fickle, interest in DIY seems set to increase indefinitely. More television programmes than ever are directed towards home improvements indirectly providing almost daily adverts for firms such as Axford's. And let's face it DIY is enjoyable: there are few more satisfying activities than planning some project however large or small then setting out to complete it oneself, buying wood and tools before spending many happy hours doing a 'proper' job. These days with the help of good materials, tools and wise

advice from firm's such as Axford's the end result is likely to be far superior to the bodges we sometimes saw our fathers do. And even if we don't always achieve quite the results we might hope for, at least even the most inept of us can enjoy once more that evocative smell of fresh sawdust and seek solace in the certain knowledge that each time we tackle such jobs we get better at them.

According to the old saying, all things change - but contrary to that general rule timber, which has been used as a building material since the dawn of history, does not look likely to be replaced in the foreseeable future.

At the beginning of the new millennium Anthony Axford Ltd was well equipped to look forward to another forty years in business with a second generation of the Axford family, Anthony's two sons, Martin and Michael, installed as directors of the firm.

This page: *Two aspects of the premises at King Street, Farnworth.*

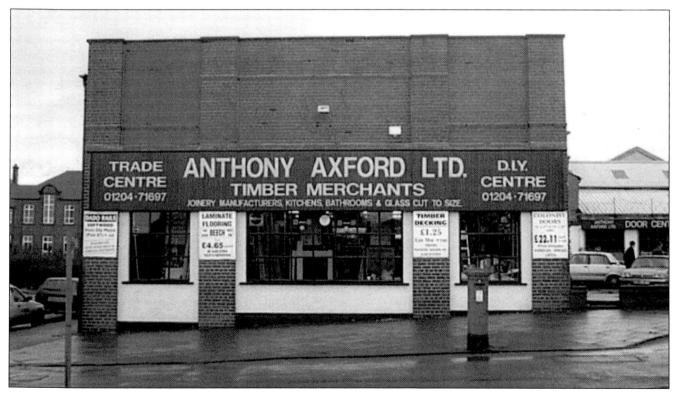